Augusta Webster

Dramatic Studies

Augusta Webster

Dramatic Studies

ISBN/EAN: 9783337340872

Printed in Europe, USA, Canada, Australia, Japan

Cover: Foto ©Thomas Meinert / pixelio.de

More available books at **www.hansebooks.com**

DRAMATIC STUDIES.

CONTENTS.

A PREACHER.

A PAINTER.

A PREACHER.

> *"Lest that by any means*
> *When I have preached to others I myself*
> *Should be a castaway."* If some one now
> Would take that text and preach to us that preach,—
> Some one who could forget his truths were old
> And what were in a thousand bawling mouths
> While they filled his—some one who could so throw
> His life into the old dull skeletons
> Of points and morals, inferences, proofs,
> Hopes, doubts, persuasions, all for time untold
> Worn out of the flesh, that one could lose from mind
> How well one knew his lesson, how oneself
> Could with another, may be choicer, style
> Enforce it, treat it from another view

And with another logic—some one warm
With the rare heart that trusts itself and knows
Because it loves—yes such a one perchance,
With such a theme, might waken me as I
Have wakened others, I who am no more
Than steward of an eloquence God gives
For others' use not mine. But no one bears
Apostleship for us. We teach and teach
Until, like drumming pedagogues, we lose
The thought that what we teach has higher ends
Than being taught and learned. And if a man
Out of ourselves should cry aloud, "I sin,
And ye are sinning, all of us who talk
Our Sunday half-hour on the love of God,
Trying to move our peoples, then go home
To sleep upon it and, when fresh again,
To plan another sermon, nothing moved,
Serving our God like clock-work sentinels,
We who have souls ourselves," why I like the rest
Should turn in anger: " Hush this charlatan
Who, in his blatant arrogance, assumes
Over us who know our duties."

                              Yet that text

Which galls me, what a sermon might be made
Upon its theme! How even I myself
Could stir some of our priesthood! Ah! but then
Who would stir me?

                    I know not how it is;
I take the faith in earnest, I believe,
Even at happy times I think I love,
I try to pattern me upon the type
My Master left us, am no hypocrite
Playing my soul against good men's applause,
Nor monger of the Gospel for a cure,
But serve a Master whom I chose because
It seemed to me I loved him, whom till now
My longing is to love; and yet I feel
A falseness somewhere clogging me. I seem
Divided from myself; I can speak words
Of burning faith and fire myself with them;
I can, while upturned faces gaze on me
As if I were their Gospel manifest,
Break into unplanned turns as natural
As the blind man's cry for healing, pass beyond
My bounded manhood in the earnestness
Of a messenger from God. And then I come

And in my study's quiet find again
The callous actor who, because long since
He had some feelings in him like the talk
The book puts in his mouth, still warms his pit
And even, in his lucky moods, himself
With the passion of his part, but lays aside
His heroism with his satin suit
And thinks "the part is good and well conceived
And very natural—no flaw to find"—
And then forgets it.
            Yes I preach to others
And am—I know not what—a castaway?
No, but a man who feels his heart asleep,
As he might feel his hand or foot. The limb
Will not awake without a little shock,
A little pain perhaps, a nip or blow,
And that one gives and feels the waking pricks.
But for one's heart I know not. I can give
No shock to make mine prick. I seem to be
Just such a man as those who claim the power
Or have it, (say, to serve the thought), of willing
That such a one should break an iron bar,
And such a one resist the strength of ten,

And the thing is done, yet cannot will themselves
One least small breath of power beyond the wont.
　　To-night now I might triumph. Not a breath
But shivered when I pictured the dead soul
Awaking when the body dies to know
Itself has lived too late, and drew in long
With yearning when I shewed how perfect love
Might make Earth's self be but an earlier Heaven.
And I may say and not be over-bold,
Judging from former fruits, "Some one to-night
Has come more near to God, some one has felt
What it may mean to love Him, some one learned
A new great horror against death and sin,
Some one at least—it may be many." Yet—
And yet—Why I the preacher look for God,
Saying "I know thee Lord, what I should see
If I could see thee as some can on earth,
But I do not see thee," and "I know thee Lord,
What loving thee is like, as if I loved,
But I cannot love thee." And even with the thought
The answer grows "Thine is the greater sin,"
And I stand self-convicted yet not shamed,
But quiet, reasoning why it should be thus,

And almost wishing I could suddenly
Fall in some awful sin, that so might come
A living sense of God, if but by fear,
And a repentance sharp as is the need.
But now, the sin being indifference,
Repentance too is tepid.

                              There are some,
Good men and honest though not overwise
Nor studious of the subtler depths of minds
Below the surface strata, who would teach,
In such a case, to scare oneself awake
(As girls do, telling ghost-tales in the dark),
With scriptural terrors, all the judgments spoken
Against the tyrant empires, all the wrath
On them who slew the prophets and forsook
Their God for Baal, and the awful threat
For him whose dark dread sin is pardonless,
So that in terror one might cling to God—
As the poor wretch, who, angry with his life,
Has dashed into a dank and hungry pool,
Learns in the death-gasp to love life again
And clings unreasoning to the saving hand.   .
Well I know some—for the most part with thin minds

Of the effervescent kind, easy to froth,
Though easier to let stagnate—who thus wrought
Convulsive pious moods upon themselves
And, thinking all tears sorrow and all texts
Repentance, are in peace upon the trust
That a grand necessary stage is past,
And do love God as I desire to love.
And now they'll look on their hysteric time
And wonder at it, seeing it not real
And yet not feigned.   They'll say "A special time
Of God's direct own working—you may see
It was not natural."
           And there I stand
In face with it, and know it. Not for me;
Because I know it, cannot trust in it;
It is not natural. It does not root
Silently in the dark as God's seeds root,
Then day by day move upward in the light.
It does not wake a tremulous glimmering dawn,
Then swell to perfect day as God's light does.
It does not give to life a lowly child
To grow by days and morrows to man's strength,
As do God's natural birthdays. God who sets

Some little seed of good in everything
May bring his good from this, but not for one
Who calmly says "*I know*—this is a dream,
A mere mirage sprung up of heat and mist;
It cannot slake my thirst : but I will try
To fool my fancy to it, and will rush
To cool my burning throat, as if there welled
Clear waters in the visionary lake,
That so perchance Heaven pitying me may send
Its own fresh showers upon me." I perchance
Might, with occasion, spite of steady will
And steady nerve, bring on the ecstasy:
But what avails without the simple faith?
I should not cheat myself, and who cheats God?
And wherefore should I count love more than truth,
And buy the loving him with such a price,
Even if 'twere possible to school myself
To an unbased belief and love him more
Only through a delusion?
                                    Not so, Lord.
Let me not buy my peace, nay not my soul,
At price of one least word of thy strong truth
Which is Thyself. The perfect love must be

When one shall *know* thee. Better one should lose
The present peace of loving, nay of trusting,
Better to doubt and be perplexed in soul
Because thy truth seems many and not one,
Than cease to seek thee, even through reverence,
In the fulness and minuteness of thy truth.

    If it be sin, forgive me: I am bold,
My God, but I would rather touch the ark
To find if thou be there than—thinking hushed
"'Tis better to believe, I will believe,
Though, were 't not for belief, 'tis far from proved"—
Shout with the people "Lo our God is there,"
And stun my doubts by iterating faith.

    And yet, I know not why it is, this knack
Of sermon-making seems to carry me
Athwart the truth at times before I know—
In little things at least; thank God the greater
Have not yet grown by the familiar use
Such puppets of a phrase as to slip by
Without clear recognition. Take to-night—
I preached a careful sermon, gravely planned,
All of it written. Not a line was meant
To fit the mood of any differing

From my own judgment : not the less I find—
(I thought of it coming home while my good Jane
Talked of the Shetland pony I must get
For the boys to learn to ride :) yes here it is,
And here again on this page—blame by rote,
Where by my private judgment I blame not.
"*We think our own thoughts on this day,*" I said,
"*Harmless it may be, kindly even, still*
"*Not Heaven's thoughts—not Sunday thoughts I'll say.*"
Well now do I, now that I think of it,
Advise a separation of our thoughts
By Sundays and by week-days, Heaven's and ours?
By no means, for I think the bar is bad.
I'll teach my children "Keep all thinkings pure,
And think them when you like, if but the time
Is free to any thinking. Think of God
So often that in anything you do
It cannot seem you have forgotten Him,
Just as you would not have forgotten us,
Your mother and myself, although your thoughts
Were not distinctly on us, while you played;
And, if you do this, in the Sunday's rest
You will most naturally think of Him;

Just as your thoughts, though in a different way,
(God being the great mystery He is
And so far from us and so strangely near),
Would on your mother's birthday-holiday
Come often back to her." But I'd not urge
A treadmill Sunday labour for their mind,
Constant on one forced round : nor should I blame
Their constant chatter upon daily themes.
I did not blame Jane for her project told,
Though she had heard my sermon, and no doubt
Ought, as I told my flock, to dwell on that.

Then here again *"the pleasures of the world*
That tempt the younger members of my flock."
Now I think really that they've not enough
Of these same pleasures. Grey and joyless lives
A many of them have, whom I would see
Sharing the natural gaieties of youth.
I wish they'd more temptations of the kind.

Now Donne and Allan preach such things as these
Meaning them and believing. As for me,
What did I mean? Neither to feign nor teach
A Pharisaic service. 'Twas just this,
That there are lessons and rebukes long made

So much a thing of course that, unobserving,
One sets them down as one puts dots to *i*'s
Crosses to *t*'s.

   A simple carelessness;
No more than that.   There's the excuse—and I,
Who know that every carelessness is falsehood
Against my trust, what guide or check have I
Being, what I have called myself, an actor
Able to be awhile the man he plays
But in himself a heartless common hack?
I felt no falseness as I spoke the trash,
I was thrilled to see it moved the listeners,
Grew warmer to my task!   'Twas written well,
Habit had made the thoughts come fluently
As if they had been real—

     Yes, Jane, yes,
I hear you—Prayers and supper waiting me—
I'll come—

   Dear Jane, who thinks me half a saint.

A PAINTER.

O 'tis completed—not an added touch
But would do mischief—and, though so far
short
Of what I aimed at, I can praise my work.
   If I, as some more fortunate men can do,
Could have absorbed my life into one task,
Could have made studies, tried effects, designed
And re-designed until some happy touch
Revealed the secret of the perfect group
In a moment's flash, could day by day have dwelt
On that one germinant theme, till it became
Memory and hope and present truth, have worked
Only upon that canvass where it grew
To the other eyes a shadow of what mine

Had seen and knew for truth, it could have been
It should have been, yes *should* have been, in the
　　teeth
Of narrow knowledge and half-tutored skill
And the impotence I chafe at of my hand
To mark my meaning, such a thing as those
Who, stooping to me, "A fair promise, sirs,
In that young man—if he'll attend to us,
The critics, he may hit the public taste
With a taking thing some day," approve the points
And count the flaws and say "For a new man
'Tis a fair picture," while they'd throw themselves
In ecstasies before some vapid peepshow
With a standard name for foreground and the rest
A clever careless toying with the brush
By a hand grown to the trick—critics forsooth
Because they have learned grammar—such a thing,
I say, as these should shrink from measuring
With blame or praise of theirs, but stand aside
And let the old ones speak, the men who worked
For something more than our great crown of art
The small green label in the corner, knew
Another public than our May-fair crowds,

Raphael and Michael Angelo and such—
Whose works sold well too. *They* should have been left
My judges whether something of the soul
That was their art had not been given me.

    Ah well I am a poor man and must earn—
And little dablets of a round-faced blonde,
Or pretty pert brunette who drops her fan,
Or else the kind the public, save the mark,
Calls poem-like, ideal, and the rest—
I have a sort of aptness for the style—
A buttercup or so made prominent
To point a moral, how youth fades like grass
Or some such wisdom, a lace handkerchief
Or broidered hem mapped out as if one meant
To give a seamstress patterns—that's to show
How "conscientious," that's the word, one is—
And a girl dying, crying, marrying, what you will,
With a blue-light tint about her—these will sell:
And they take time, and if they take no thought
Weary one over much for thinking well.
A man with wife and children, and no more
To give them than his hackwork brings him in,
Must be a hack and let his masterpiece

Go to the devil.

                Well my masterpiece,
As to the present, is achieved at last;
But by what straining of a wearied hand
And wearied eyes and wearied aching head
Worn with the day's forced work! And now I come
And fold my arms before it, and play the judge,
And am, though not content, yet proud of it.
And after all what is it? So much width.
Of my best canvass made unserviceable,
Spoilt for the dablets, so much time defrauded
From my tradesman work. What will it gain for me?
And why I do not answer at first blush
Just "disappointment," is that I have grown
Too used to disappointment now to set
A hope on any issue. I shall hear
My work observed with vacant hems and has,
And a slur of timorous praise. And I shall see
A quiet face or two light up with thought—
And these, although perhaps they think no more
Of the painter or his work nor care to keep
Remembrance of my unfamiliar name,
Will be my friends for the moment, and will note

With a sort of kind regret where I fall short.
And some severer connoisseur will fume:
"Now here's a man with a certain faculty.
The more shame for him! Were he some schooled
        drudge
Doing his best one would forgive the fault.
But here's a harebrained fellow comes to us
'I am a painter I—no need to study—
Here's genius at my back—splash, dash away—
I'll win a fortune and a name at once,
And deserve them bye and bye?' He ought to take
Two or three years at least of study, draw
More than he paints, scan how the masters did it,
Go to school in Rome. But no, his vanity
Pats his genius on the back. Pooh! He descend
To dull apprentice plodding! He take time
Before he paints for the world!—Fie on it though
To see a man so sin against his gift."
And then another says "Yes he should wait,"
And another "Wait," and "Wait," and once more
        "Wait."
Out on them fools! Do they know a man may die
Waiting? Waiting, when waiting means to starve

Do they think of that?

        What Ruth, my pretty one,
Come to learn what's my trouble? Startle you,
Did I with sudden steps and speaking loud?
'Tis nothing, dearest—only the old tale
That you and I keep fretting at, what cross
And spirit-killing work it is to slave
At these man-wasting trifles day by day,
Cutting one's life in mess-pieces, and see
No better chance for freedom than to cheat
The fashionable world that chatters art
By some chance masterpiece into paying one
Enough to buy the time to wait and learn.
And then the critics say " You should have waited.
'Tis the fault of the age, our young men will not
    wait. "
And the fashionable world says "To be sure—
The fault of the age!   Indeed he should have waited:
We might have bought his pictures then:" and flies
With open purse, on a race for who bids first,
To its latest darling's studio—takes all there,
If he did it awake, or sleeping, or by proxy,
At equal price. What matter?   There's his name!

Ah Ruth! If I could only win a name!
And then, love, then!

For I know there is in me
Another power than what men's eyes yet find
In these poor works of mine. But who can tell
If now I ever shall become myself?
My one believer, I have learned from you
To use that phrase: but what is a man's self
Excepting what he is, what he has learned
And what he does? You make it what he hopes.
Well love, persuade me with your earnest voice
And look of long belief, this twentieth time—
Persuade me that the day we hope must come,
Because it is myself. I am worn out,
Sick to the heart. I need your love so much.
Talk to me love; find fault; dispute with me,
With smiles and kisses ready all the while,
And your dear arms clinging to me; prophesy,
You happy prophet who can fill your eyes
With sunshine and see brightness where you will.
And come now, find me in my picture there
Something to praise; I can believe your praise
Although you love me.

No you cannot stay—

Yes, yes, I hear the summons. If Blanche cries—
Poor Ruth! I could be jealous of your care
For the children, were it not so hard to me
To see you forced to play the handmaid to them.
Come back when the child sleeps.

                              Going she leaves
A darkness after her.   Ruth, but for you
I could not paint a sunbeam, could not bear
To have a happy thought look out on me
From my own canvass : now because of you
I do not envy brightness.

                        Yet she says
And, I fear me, almost thinks it, my poor wife,
"If I had never come to burden you,
You might have won your way by now."   Ah well,
A sunless way without her, yet perhaps
It is a true sad word.   I might have been
Without her what she'd have me be.

                              No, no—
A handier painter possibly, more apt
With nice true touches and the fearless brush
Exact without restraint, most certainly
A more successful man, but not the man

My earnest Ruth believes in. Darling, you
Who, under all your pretty fitful ways,
Your coaxings and your poutings, have the strength
Of the noblest kind of women, helping strength
For any man with worth enough to use it—
You keep me to the level of my hopes :
I shall not fall beneath them while you live.
It was a good day for me when you came
Into my fretted life, and I thank God
It was no evil one for you. Dear wife,
If you had been one born to pleasant things,
Cared for and praised in a familiar home,
Not knowing what it is to say, "Well this
Costs sixpence, I can do without," and "This
Is marked a penny and will serve the turn"—
If you had had one other in the world
To take up your dead father's guardianship
And watch a little for you, then long since
I should have cursed myself who brought you here
To live on empty hopes and drudge the while.
But you are happier even in our want
And your enduring than you would have been
Still pining, smiling, on, the mere fed slave

Of a cross idiot and her hoyden brats.
You were a fool, the mistress-creature thought,
To leave the comfort she had graciously
Designed to keep you in some half score years,
Raised salary and so forth, for a home
So poor as I yet had to give. But you
Still said "It will be Home" and you and I
Knew something, even then, by hope or instinct
Of the meaning of that common word which she
Poor soul, among her gewgaw drawing-rooms
Had never dreamed of. You are happy, love;
We have our many troubles, many doubts,
We are at war with fate and a hard world,
And God knows whether we shall overcome;
But you are happy, love, because you know
You are my happiness.

　　　　　　　　And I might say,
In the bitterness of these dull wearing days,
While like that poor caged squirrel in the street
I beat my ceaseless way and gain no step,
I have no other left me, were it not
That, even at this moment, the warm glow
Of yellow evening sunshine brightening down

Upon the red geraniums she has placed
To feast my eyes with colour, bringing out
That line of shadow deeper on the wall,
With the exquisite half lights thrown from those white
        folds,
Softer than mists at sundawn, gladden me
With the old joy and make me know again
How one can live on beauty and be rich
Having only that—a thing not hard to find,
For all the world is beauty. We know that
We painters, we whom God shows how to see.
We have beauty ours, we take it where we go.
Aye my wise critics, rob me of my bread,
You can do that, but of my birthright no.
Imprison me away from skies and seas
And the open sight of earth and her rich life
And the lesson of a face or golden hair:
I'll find it for you on a whitewashed wall
Where the slow shadows only change so much
As shows the street has different darknesses
At noontime and at twilight.
                Only that
Could make me poor of beauty which I dread

Sometimes, I know not why, save that it is
The one thing which I could not bear, not bear
Even with Ruth by me, even for Ruth's sake—
If this perpetual plodding with the brush
Should blind my fretted eyes.

                    Would the children starve,
Poor pretty playthings who have not yet learned
That they are poor? And Ruth—

                    Well, baby sleeps?
Ah love, you come in time to chase some thoughts
I do not care to dwell on. Come, stand there
And criticise my picture. It has failed
Of course—I always fail. Yet on the whole
I think the world would praise it were I known.

JEANNE D'ARC.

SISTER ANNUNCIATA.

JEANNE D'ARC.

TO me—to me! Dunois! La Hire! Old Daulon,
Thou at the least shouldst stand by me—Oh
haste!
The soul of France is in me, rescue me!—
Turn back the flyers—Cowards, have you learned
These English car. be conquered, yet you flee?
To me!—Oh! I am wounded! Oh! this time
We shall not sleep in Paris—

What is this?

Is this not Paris but sieged Compiegne?
Back, to the fort! This once we needs must fly.
In, in! They are closing on us— in!—Oh Christ!
The gate drops down! And I without, alone!
Open, the foe is on me. Help! Oh now

I feel I am a woman and 'mong foes!
Oh save me!—

      Oh you blessed saints of Heaven,
Do you come down to me again? You smile
A wondrous holiness, ineffable.
Oh what a brightness stars upon your brows!
It grows—it grows! I see you clearly now,
You who first sent me forth, and all this while
Have nerved me to be forward 'mid these men
Who press to carnage as a lightsome girl
Hastens her steps to where the dancers wait;
You who have warned me, counselled, comforted,
Given me persuasion and the gift to awe
And the strong soldier spirit of command;
My guardians and consolers, who, beyond
All other saints, have taken part for me,
Me and my France—St Catherine, thou pure
Thou holy bride, and brave St Margaret.

    You bring me peace, dear saints, and I had
      need:
Oh help me from myself and these mad dreams.
Oh hear me, I have had most fearful visions:
I thought I fought before the walls of Paris

And did not conquer—Oh the agony
Even to dream of that first shamed defeat!—
And then the dream was shifted: I was thronged
By furious enemies before the gate
Of Compiegne, and taken prisoner!
They were haling me along, and still I strove,
And strove, and strove. And all the while it seemed
As if by an awful prescience I knew
My waiting death, more dreadful than to lie
Shattered and gashed beneath the onward rush
Of the frantic horses spurred into our ranks,
And die amid the roar of English shouts—
Meseemed my living limbs were to be given
To scorch and writhe and shrivel in the fire—
I was to know like torment and like shame
With those who front our God with blasphemies
And loathsome magic—Ah! my head swims round
Still dizzy with the terror of my dream.

But you are come, you gracious messengers,
To chase the troubled visions that the Fiend
Tortures me with. Stay with me for awhile,
And let me feel your mystic influence
Thrill all my being into rapt delight:

Then I shall feel in me a threefold strength,
And go forth eager in the morn, athirst
For the madness of the battle and the flush
Of conquest and the pride of leadership,
Go forth, as I am wont, to victory.

     Oh you are dimmer!—Woe! woe! was my dream
But a confused remembering in sleep?
Where you were standing do I see the moonlight
Falling on prison-walls? Oh! I have waked
From the bewilderings of cruel sleep
To dreadful sharp reality. Woe! woe!
The chains are heavy on me! I am lost!

     But which is dream then? For it seemed to me
I woke, as I have often waked at night
From troubled fancies, and I saw those Holy
Who lead me, and my heart leaped with the thought
That I should raise the fortunes of our France
Yet higher in the coming fight. Yes surely
We give battle in the morning, surely they,
Those holy ones, they warned me even now.
They would not mock me. This must be the dream:
These chains, this prison, they must be the dream.

     Oh Mother of the Blessed, hear me; come

Down from thy throne ringed round about with angels,
Come from His side, that Holy One, our Christ,
And comfort me with love, and show me truth.
Oh! come, ye virgin saints, and teach me here,
A poor weak girl, lone in my helplessness,
Crying to you for that once strength you gave.

    They come—Lady of Heaven, it is thou!
Oh! Mary-Mother, blessed among women,
For thy life's sorrow's sake deliver me
In this distress: Oh! show me which is truth.

    The vision grows. Oh look! they show me all
My true career!—I see it—Yes, my home
In the far village. Those were dreamy days,
And pleasant till the visions made me know
My higher destiny and I grew restless
In the oppressive quiet. Waning—Gone!
Ah well, I would have lost a longer while
Gladly in that kind dreaming****Yes, my king,
So did he honour me when I declared him
Among his courtiers****Yes, so Orleans fell—
Oh! my brave glory! yes *I* beat them back,
These Englishmen that were invincible!****
Yes, so I set the crown upon his head

In sacred Rheims. Oh noble! how the crowd,
Eager to kiss my vesture, touch me, throngs
Around me, me a simple peasant girl
Made first of women and of warriors
In all our France!—Hush, hush, vainglorious heart,
How often have the voices chidden thee
For thy too arrogant delight! Not mine
The honour, but the Lord's who sent me forth.
I a mean herd-wench from the fields—what more?
But made God's instrument, to show Himself
And not the power of man conquers for France,
How dare I boast? Oh! was it for this fault,
This foolish fault of pride, that check was sent?
What needs this vision of it? But too well
I keep the memory of that first shame,
My first defeat. Yes, Paris, I still fire
With angry blushes at thy name****And this—
Oh! but my brain whirls—whirls—what is it? Cloud
And dull confusion. Who is it that stands
Mouthing and gecking at me? Why now, Pierre,
Because, forsooth, thou art our neighbour's son,
Must I be bound to dance with thee at will?
Why flout me with so stale a grudge, my friend?

Is the face changed? It was Dame Madelon's Pierre,
The poor good clumsy youth, whose suits and sulks
Had so passed from my mind, I thought I saw.
And now—I know it, the long fiendish sneer,
The sudden glare! Ah! so the vision grows
Perfect again. A trial call they this?
A pastime rather for their lordly hearts;
They bait the tethered prey before they kill.
Is it Christian, my lord bishop, so to taunt me,
Me innocent and helpless?—Ah! I look
But on a vision: I am here alone;
In prison and condemned! Ah me! the dreams,
They did not mock me. This then is the truth,
The prison and the chains—Christ! and the death!
    Stay yet with me ye blessed.
                        They are gone!
They touched my forehead with their martyr palms;
And the dear Heaven-Mother smiled on them,
And the same smile on *me*. But they are gone,
And I am left unaided to my fate.
    Was it for this that I was chosen out,
From my first infancy—marked out to be
Strange 'mid my kindred and alone in heart,

Never to cherish thoughts of happy love
Such as some women know in happy homes,
Laying their heads upon a husband's breast,
Or singing, as the merry wheel whirrs round,
Sweet cradle songs to lull their babes to sleep?
Was it for this that I forbore to deck
My beauty with the pleasant woman arts
That other maidens use and are not blamed,
Hid me in steel, and for my chaplet wore
A dented helmet on my weary brows?
Ah! I like other women might have lived
A home-sweet life in happy lowly peace,
And France had not been free but I content,
A simple woman only taking thought
For the kind drudgery of household cares.
But I obeyed the visions: I arose,
And France is free—And I ere the next sun
Droops to the west shall be a whitened mass—
Dead ashes on the place where the wild flames
Shot up—Oh horrible!

          Oh! God, my God,
Dost thou behold, and shall these men, unjust,
Slay me, thy servant? Oh! and shall my name

Be muttered low hereafter in my France,
A sorceress and one impure?

                    They say
I commune with the Fiend and he has led
My way so high. Yes, if he could do this,
And I, deserted as I am of God,
Might cease to war with him and buy my life,
And greatness—and revenge!—

                        Oh God! forgive.
I sin. Oh deadliest sin of all my life!
Oh! pardon! pardon! Oh! have I condemned
My soul to everlasting fire by this?
My brain whirls—whirls—Forgive!

                        Oh see they come,
They touch me with their palms! She smiles again,
The holy Mother! Yes, they beckon me.
Now they are vanished in a cloud of light.
I shall not see them more: but I shall know
They will hold fast my trembling soul in death
And bear me to my home—a better home
Than earth has given me.

                    The dawn begins.
How fast the hours leap on towards the end!—

Will the pain wring me long? Ah me! that fire!
They might have given me a gentler death.

 The sound of footsteps! They are coming now.
No, they pass on—No, now they are at the door.
They are coming to pursue me to the last;
They will mock me once again with promises,
To buy from me the whiteness of my name
And have me blast it by my own last lie.
No matter; now they cannot bait me long.

 My God, I thank Thee who hast chosen me
To be Thy messenger to drive them forth:
And, since my death was destined with the mission,
Lord of my life, I thank Thee for my death.

SISTER ANNUNCIATA.

I. AN ANNIVERSARY.

My wedding day! A simple happy wife,
Stolen from her husband's sight a little while
To think how much she loved him, might so kneel
Alone with God and love a little while,
(For if the Church bless love, is love a sin?)
And, coming back into the happy stir
Of children keeping the home festival,
Might bring the Heaven's quiet in her heart;
Yes, even coming to him, coaxing him
With the free hand that wears his fetter on it,
Sunning her boldly in his look of love,
And facing him with unabashed fond eyes

Might, being all her husband's, still be God's
And know it—happy with no less a faith
Than we who, ever serving at His shrine,
Know ourselves His alone.

                     Am I sinning now
To think it? Nay, no doubt I went too far:
The bride of Christ is more than other women;
I must not dare to even such to me.
They have their happiness, I mine; but mine
Is it not of Heaven heavenly, theirs of earth,
And therefore tainted with earth's curse of sin?
Did Mary envy Martha? Oh my Lord
Forgive thy handmaid if her spirit lone,
A little lone because the clog of flesh
That sunders it from Thee still burdens it
With the poor human want of human love,
Hungry a moment and by weakness snared,
Has dared, with the holy manna feast in reach,
To think on Egypt's fleshpots and not loathe.
Oh! Virgin Mother, pray thou for thy child,
That I who have escaped the dangerous world,
Rising above it on thy altar steps,
May feel the heavens round me lifting me,

Lifting me higher, higher, day by day,
Until the glory blinds me, and my ears
Hear only Heaven's voices, and my thoughts
Have passed into one blending with His will,
And earth's dulled memories seem nothingness!

　　Ah me! poor soul, even here 'tis a hard fight
With the wiles of Satan! Was the Abbess wise
To set me, in the night too when one most
Is tempted to let loose forbidden dreams
And float with them back to the far-off life
Of foolish old delights,—yes, was she wise
To set me in the night-hush such a watch,
Wherein "to think upon my ancient life
With all its sins and follies, and prepare
To keep my festival for that good day
That wedded me out of the world to Christ?"
She has forgotten doubtless, 'tis so long
Since she came here, how, trying to recall
Girl sins and follies, some things of the past
Might be recalled too tenderly, and so
The poisonous sad sweet sin of looking back
Steal on one unawares.
　　　　　　Oh hush! alas

How easy 'tis to sin ! Now I have tripped;
Obedience must not question.   But one learns
With every hour of growing holiness
How bitter Satan is against the Saints.
I muse if I, who of the sisterhood
Am surely, now that Agatha is dead,
The nearest saintly practice, most in prayer,
And most in penance, crucifying most
The carnal nature, till they point to me
With pride for the convent and some envy too
For themselves left lower in the race—if I
Am tripped so often, how then fare the rest ?
Though doubtless Satan does not track so close
Until he fears one.   But they are less armed :
Alas how he may break them ! Poor weak souls,
How I shall pray for them : for bye and bye,
Doubtless, I shall be freer from the self
I have yet to guard, my victory will be won
And I shall tread on sin, invulnerable,
As the Saints do at last.
                              If I, that is,
Might reach the goal I strain at, the one goal
Ambition may seek sinless—though I faint

The goal I *will* attain. I think in truth
My feet are on the road, and, let them bleed
Among the thorns, I still press on.

                              Perhaps
It is because she sees how strong I grow,
She gave me this ordeal, this the first year-day,
Out of the several, she has risked it. No.
She'd not have tried one of the others thus;
She sees I shall not fail. I cannot think,
Although she knows me her successor here,
She plans to lessen me from a renown
Of sanctity that bids to dwindle hers.
No—she is kind, there is no seeming in it,
And simply good, although no miracle
Of self-set discipline, and her meek mind
Would find a daughter's merit glorying
The convent's name glory enough for her—
She is my friend.

                    Ah! I remember me
In the first days—when I was sad and restless
And seemed an alien in a hopeless world,
All form and pious parrot-talk, a home
For stunting dull despair shut from the sun,

A nursery to bloat the sick self in
To a mis-shapen God to fēed whose fires
The loves and hopes and faiths, the very life
Of the young heart must perish, and I knew
For the best future nothing but a blank,
For then the present bitterness of death,
The horrible death in life—my first belief
In any comfort earlier than the grave's
Came from a touch of tenderness in her,
Only a tone, a look as she passed by
Where I was sitting by the broken well,
Looking at the green growth that overslimed
The never heaven waters, thinking "this,
The image of the thing my life becomes,
Unlighted, unlightgiving, ignorant
Of sunflash and of shadow, with the slime
Of utter foul stagnation hiding heaven
As surely as its narrow walls fair earth,
And under all, chill, chill!" "God bless you daughter,"
She said; her usual greeting, but it came
With the kind of sound one likes to dwell upon—
A little trivial phrase in the right tone
Makes music for so long. "God bless you daughter"

As if she meant it—and there was the touch
Of a mere womanly pity in her eyes.
So her blessing loosed the bands about my heart,
And the passion of tears broke out.

                       'Twas the first time
Since the night before they brought me to my vows
In a passive dream; I think because since then
I had been hopeless, and it must have been
That the feeling of a human tenderness
Still folding me, made something like a hope,
Feeding my withering heart like water drops
Given the poor plant brought from the fresh free air
And natural dewings of the skyward soil,
Where its wild growth took bent at the wind's will,
To learn indoors an artificial bloom
Or die. Before it had been too near death
For weeping—And the comfort of those tears!
I almost wish that I could weep so now!

    No, no, I take again my wish, which was a sin;
It was no wish, a fancy at the most;
Lord, let it not be numbered with my sins!

    What mere mad sin against the spirit, that,
If I could wish to lose my hard-won state

Of holy peace. And wherefore should I weep?
For what endurance? I who have inhaled
The rich beatitude of my spousalship,
To the heart's core.

            But *then* I only saw
The human side, knew but the present loss
Of the outer bloom of life, and did not know
That, stripped of the flower-wings, the fruit grew on,
Yea, and to ripe to immortality,
In this sure shelter. Or I knew it, say,
As I know that bye and bye, when I am dead,
I shall be sunned in the grave on summer days,
While, if one now were standing in the frosts,
The chariest winter beam were something, all;
And what such summers waiting for the time
Of silence and of change? A sorry mocking
Of hungering hope with bitter dead sea fruit.

    She preached to me, good woman, when she
        turned,
Catching the breath of my outswelling grief,
And, with the softened smile some mothers rest
Upon their children, came to me quietly,
And sat beside me there. No doubt she ran

Her whole small simple round of eloquence;
I have heard it all since then, I think; but then
I did not hear—a murmur in my ears
That hummed on, soothing, like a lullaby.
And through it I perceived some scraps of texts,
And godly phrases, and examples drawn
From the lives of the saints, and wise encourage-
      ments;
And I wept on. But the warm touch of her hands
Nursing my right hand in them motherly,
And the feeling of her kindly neighbourhood,
These spoke a language that I understood
And thrilled to in my desolate mood. Through them
That heavy sense of prison loneliness,
Whether I moved alone or companied,
Was lifted from my heart, broken away
In the rushing of my tears; and even from then,
Wherefore I know not, I was moved to grope
Up from the dark towards the light of Heaven.

But ah the long ascent! It was enough
At first to learn the patience that subdued
My throbbing heart to its new quiet rule,
The hope of Heaven that bore down earth's despair—

But these were comfort, and the craving grew
As natural for them as the sick man's
For the pain-soothing draught he learned perforce
To school his palate to. But then the effort
To be another self, to know no more
The fine-linked dreams of youth, the flying thoughts
Like sparkles on the wave-tops changing place
And all one scattered brightness, the high schemes
And glorious wild endeavours after good,
Fond, bubble-soaring, but how, beautiful!
The sweet unreal reveries, the gush
Of voiceless songs deep in the swelling heart,
The dear delight of happy girlish hopes—
Of, ah my folly! some hopes too strange sweet
That I dare think of them even to rebuke—
Ah not to be forgotten though they lie
Too deep for even memory. Alas!
Even if I would, how could I now recall
To their long-faded forms those phantasies
Of a far, other, consciousness which now
Beneath the ashes of their former selves
Lie a dead part of me, but still a part,
Oh evermore a part.

I do not think

There can be sin in that, in knowing it.

I am not nursing the old foolish love

Which clogged my spirit in those bitter days.

Ah no, dear as it was even in its pain,

I have trampled on it, crushed its last life out.

I do not dread the beautiful serpent now;

It cannot breathe again, not if I tried

To warm it at my breast, it is too dead

And my heart has grown too cold; the Lord himself,

I thank Him, has renewed it virgin-cold

To give to Him. I do but recognize

A simple truth, that that which has been lived,

Lived down to the deeps of the true being, *is*

Even when past for ever, has become

Inseparable from the lifelong self:

But yet it lives not with the *present* life.

So, in this wise, I may unshamed perceive

That the dead life, that the dead love, are still

A part of me.

           Nay do I fool myself?

Why do I fever so thinking of him?

Why do I think of him? What brought his face

So vividly before me? Angelo,
Art thou in the night-stillness waking now
Remembering me, remembering me who came
A little moment into thy bright life
And seemed to make it brighter, and then passed,
Leaving no doubt a little cloud behind,
Till when? Till now? Till death comes with the end?
Or till the other's smile had lighted it
With the rich rose of dawn to brighter day?
While she lies dreaming of the dainty dress
Ordered for next night's ball, art thou indeed
Thinking, alone in heart, of former days,
And asking the dull hush to speak of me?
Or is it but a careless memory
Passing thy dreamy thought a moment long,
A wondering lightly "Is she reconciled
To the lot they gave her?" But, whate'er it be,
Surely some thought of thine came to me now
And called mine to thee.

                Nay, it must not be.
Oh once my own beloved, now a mere name,
A name of something that one day was dear,
In an old world, to one who is no more,

Vex me no more with idle communings,—
Love me, love her, what matters it to me?
I stand as far apart as angels are
From earthly passion—not by my own strength,
But by the grace shewn in me, and the bar
Of my divine espousal. Stand far off
Even in thought.

            Yes, though this was thy word,
That long fond evening when we stole apart
Out of the music and the talking, when
We stood below the orange-boughs abloom,
And the sweet night was silent, and the waves
Were rocking softly underneath the moon,
Asleep in the white calm, and we, alone,
Were whispering all our hearts each into each:
"Eva, my Eva, darling of my life,
If they should part us still you are my all.
I will not love the other. She might bear
My name, gild with the purchase money for it
Our houses' tarnished splendours, rear the heirs
Of its new greatness.—You, you, only you,
In your cold prison, would be wife to me,
Wife of my soul. Are we not one, love, so?

They could not beat down that; and I would live
In a secret world with you, so that in Heaven
I could claim you boldly, 'this was my own wife'
And all the angels know it true."

                                        Ah me!
How long that wild rapt promise hindered me
In my first struggles for the Saints' cold peace,
Because he spoke it in a certain tone—
Sometimes he used it—that had a strange power
To thrill me with strange pleasure through and
        through
And leave long after echoes still possessed
Of something more than most tones, even his,
And easier to recall at will; and these
Remained with me; I could not quite forego
Their dangerous sweetness. So the Tempter came
Saying always "He too thinks of them" and I
Would be so weak, so wicked, that I thought,
"I cannot try to be in perfectness
One of the Heavenly Brides, lest I succeed
And, standing white-robed with the virgin train
Who in the after kingdom follow Christ,
See him and know him and am lost to him,

Even there where the last hope was."
                                        But now,
No more my love for ever, now at length
In this more perfect day of my raised soul,
I can say calmly: "Though this was thy word
I do not bid thee honour it." It was
The dream of a mad moment, let it pass:
I would not hold thee to it if I could:
I scale a heavenward height, and if I shiver
A little, just a little, in the snows,
On the darker days, should I for this descend
Into the earth-balmed valley and forego
The victories of my toiling steps, the crown
Of my long enterprize! No, though thy voice
Were thrice and thrice as eager-sweet as when
Long since it said "be mine in earth" to say
"Be mine in heaven" I could not wait for thee.
I go alone, wearing my spousal ring,
My bridal throne is ready.
                            But, although
I love thee now with only such a love
As a dead saint might love that looked from Heaven,
It is no sin that I should yearn for thee

That thou mightst also rise and lift thyself
Out from the world, leaving its honeyed wines
That overglad the heart, its corn and oil,
For the barren mountain-summit near God's stars,
In the cold pure air where the earth's growths dwine
  off,
Leaving the joys of common life, the pride,
The beauty and the love ; perceiving nought
Except the goal of such a holiness
As I would bid thee strive for. Ah ! my brother,
If this might be, and we two, though apart,
Were one in such an aim !
      But can I tell
If thou art Angelo whom once I knew ?
She with her silly beauty, smiling forth
The brightness of her self-complacency
Till one might easily be taken in
And fancy she'd at least just so much heart
As served to wish one well with—may she not
By now have dazzled thee or flattered thee
Till thou hast given her thy heart for plaything—
All she could make of it ! It might be so:
For there *were* times, when thou and I, poor children,

Were chafing impotent while stronger hands
Made havoc of our simple lovers' plot,
That I half jealous, though I doubted not
Thy inmost faith to me, thought piteously:
"Ah but for the marvellous gold of those loose curls,
And the glitter of those crystal-brown strange eyes
Perfect in sudden glances and drooped coyness,
He might have made them know the task too hard
To bend him to their scheming."
      Yes, I feared,
Even while I said: "I wrong him by the thought"
My own own lover, like the warriors
In some old fight I knew of ere the lore
Of secular things grew babble talk to me,
Was dazzled in the eyes by the strong sun,
The sun that was her beauty, and so fought
As if in the dark and vainly.
      Could it be?
I do not think it. In the days of love
One doubts because one loves, because one knows
One is too willing to be credulous:
But, now that there is no sweet weakness left
To daze my judgment, I can vouch for him.

He, having, in the teeth of interest
And the worldly prudence preached from both our
      homes,
Chosen me to love, me with a mind and soul
And woman's worth enough on me to love
In something more than pretty kitten's play;
Me with some dusky beauty of my own—
If in all else made less by hers yet more,
I think, to those who care to see a life
Shew through the breathing mask, more by the
      power
(Mine and not hers let her be earth's most fair)
To steal from gazing eyes the accurate sense
Of parts and shapings of it and to leave
"The long impression"—thus he imaged it—
"Of a beauty like the sky's on some rare eve,
When glow and shadow, and the luminous change
Of perfeƈt-blended yet contrasted dyes,
And blueness of the ether, make a oneness
Of something higher than the different names
We fit to different kinds of beauty hold
A meaning for; and we can only feel
The soul-deep influence, and cannot scan

The several parts, nor say 'the best is there'
Nor 'I have seen sometimes a richer rose,
One morn a purer gold'; nor can retain
A perfect presence of it, but retain
Mid the deep memories that build up lives,
Though out of sight beneath and overlapped
By the hiding Present, a long consciousness
Of something known beyond mere perfectness."
He, prizing me at this, he, knowing me
In my true self, and knowing that I loved him,
Could he turn patiently to a mere face,
A mere most lovely dainty-blossomed face
And statue-moulded body––only this?
Nothing to meet him in his higher moods;
Nothing to rise with him from the dull round
Of the drudging daily self; nothing to hold
The overflowings of his deeper soul;
No mind in which to measure his grave thoughts;
No thoughts with which to swell them. Could he drop
From the proud height of my love to such as hers,
Unconscious of the fall and well-content?
No: time may have perchance, (tho' for his sake
I cannot hope it), levelled down to her

His husband's heart, but that were but the fret
And gradual moulding of the many days,
And over-mastering custom: *she* had never
That triumph on me.

                Though my mother once,
(Breaking the shadowy twilight where I sat
Lest she should see me weep, with flouting light,
And the sad quiet of my lonely thoughts
With most unwonted icy comforting),
Bade me believe, because she had the proofs,
Or almost proofs, that Angelo was glad
To be compelled to her whom he would call
Even in my hearing 'Fairest of the roses'
And, though he prized me in a certain sort
For the memory of a boyhood's rash first love
And out of kindness to my love for him,
It was perceived by those who knew him best—
Nay more was growing common talk to them—
That his fancy for me palled apace and love
For the bright Giulia overmastered quite
The stress he put to hide it for the sake
Of humouring my weakness to the last,
And saving me from scorn's deriding finger

That mocks the maiden who is true too long.
She said it, yes, just in such sudden words,
Unwavering : but I, did I believe ?
Too much was said ; no doubt a little less,
An inference, a little sharp-barbed hint
Touching my sometimes fears and making them
More real to me, might have served the need ;
But such a tale was idle as the threats
Of the outside wind wild-storming in the dark
To one who sleeps well-housed. Why, all the more
Because he never shrank from giving praise
To that most evident beauty though I heard,
I knew what worth the pretty plaything's smiles
Were counted at in his more earnest moods.
She touch his heart ! my very bitterest fears
Were that his mere man's fancy might be caught,
And harm be done before the cloying came.

You did but anger me, proud mother mine,
With your pretended soothings. Was it worth,
Having queened it for so many frigid years
Over your daughters' lives and never once
Stooped to a little pet word, or a kiss
Beyond the formal seal that stamped receipt

Of our daily homage paid, or just a look
To shew you knew what mother-loving meant—
Was it worth to come down from your pedestal
At the last moment thus to play the part
Of a mere common woman softening down
Her girl's weak grief at fate inevitable?
You could not do it either; for your talk
Of sorrow and of sympathy was such
As singing might be coming from one deaf
But newly learning speech by watching lips.

    Yet, maybe, at the last she felt some pang,
Maybe, altho' she would not change her purpose—
Could not perhaps—our uncle has some power
I think, beyond advising, in the house
He rules with her by such an iron rod,
And, once our destinies mapped out by him
What human will, what human suffering
Could alter them? "We have concluded thus"—
Swelling himself in the authority
Of priestly greatness and of guardianship;
"We have concluded thus"—and then my mother
Would nod assent, and what remained to us
His brother's children, hers, but mute submission?

But she, maybe, the parting near, was moved,
The mother-heart in her touched thro' the frosts
Long custom had clogged round it; or else why
Should she at all have tried to mould my will
Into content? She might have kept her height
Of questionless command: what mattered it
If I should fret or no? Thus stood the case :
There were too many daughters in our home,
Too scanty portioning, and, with a name
So high as ours, need was that none should wed
But with the other noblest houses : then
It must not be that one of the three sons
Should be too poor to bear up from the dust
The honour of his heirship of long race:
And where were dowers for such brides, and where
Gold purses for the spending of such sons?
At least one dower might be saved, one girl
Must choose the cloister. Who but Eva then?
Eva·who, wise with fifteen years of life,
Had recognized her call to saintly life:
Eva who, in her folly of eighteen,
Had chosen for herself such a mad match,
Impossible, with one even as herself

Of an impoverished house, whose princely kin
Wise-judging knew the pair must never wed
And had a richer bride in hand for him.
What mattered it if I said 'yea' or 'nay'
'It likes me' or 'it likes me not'?   There stood
The argument, could weeping alter it,
Or a girl's angers?   Why should she have cared
To set herself a task so out of wont,
Unless she felt some yearning to her child
And fain would have me sorrow something less
And go from her in peace?

                      Yes, I will think
You did mean kindness and the comforting
That angered pride might give me in my need.
But, mother, had you known a little more
Of your child's heart, of any human heart,
You would have known what bitter death in life
Your words believed would bring me, stabbing me
With the last despair of scorning while I loved.

    And, since you could not fail to recognize
Something of your own pride retraced in me,
I marvel you saw not how you must rouse
Its strength against belief with such a tale.

A meek prompt faith! for the blowing of some breaths
Of "thus they say"s to think oneself so slight
As to be brushed off like a clinging burr,
Shaken into the mud beneath his feet
By the man one honoured with one's whole of love!
And more, I marvel that you did not feel
" Her Angelo is out of reach of scorn,
And she could not believe unless she scorned,"
And know untried the vainness of your talk.

    Oh, only love, I never broke my truth
By questionings of yours, and you, I know,
Had in me that blind trust that was my right—
And yet we are apart. Oh! it is hard!
Has God condemned all love except of Him?
Will He have only market marriages
Or sprung from passion fancies soon worn out,
Lest any two on earth should partly miss
The anger and distrust that haunt earth's homes
And cease to know there is no calm till death?

    None for who lives the outside waking life:
We are calm here, calm enough. Oh Angelo
Why am I here in the ceaseless formal calm
That makes the soul swell to one bursting self

And seem the whole great universe, the while
It only sees itself, learns of itself,
Hopes for itself, feeds, preys upon itself
And not one call comes to it from without
" Think of me too, a little live for me,
Take me with thee in growing nearer God"?
Why am I—?

       Am I mad? Am I mad? I rave
Some blasphemy which is not of myself!
What is it? Was there a demon here just now
By me, within me? Those were not my thoughts
Which just were thought or spoken—which was it?
Oh not my thoughts, not mine! All saints of heaven
Be for me, answer for me; I am yours,
I am your Master's, how can I be Satan's?
I have not lost my soul by the wild words.
Not yet, not yet.

       Oh this was what I feared.
The night-watch is a long one and I flag,
My head is hot, I feel the fever fire
Of weariness before the languor comes.
I am left prey to Satan's snares for those
Who too much live again the former life

In the dangerous times of unwatched loneliness.
He lurks in those retrodden paths, he makes
His snaky coils of all these memories,
Clogging them round my spirit. Is the work
Of long long months, of years, undone in a night?

    Alas! the ordeal is too hard for me.
I am shut out in the dark! where is the oil
To feed the virgin's lamp? What! are these tears
Only of water? They should be of blood
Fitter to weep my sin in.

                I will wait;
I cannot gather those old histories.
My mind is wandering. I cannot tell
How far I went, nay, if I had begun.
I cannot think. But I can weep and pray.
Surely I may break thus much the command
And yet obey. Oh I may stop to pray
And to repent. Oh I *may* weep and pray,
So broken as I am. All saints of Heaven
Pray with me, for me, pray or I am lost.
I lost! I lost! Heaven's mercy on me, lost!

    *   *   *   *   *   *

    Have I slept? But no, I think I was in prayer

5

The whole time that I knelt—unless indeed
A little heavy moment at the last;
It is too chill for sleep.   How strange and grey
The morning glimmers! What an awful thing,
Although one feels not why, the silence is
When the new creeping light treads on the dark
Like a white mist above it, and beside
Its leaden pallor hollow blacknesses
Lurk, shifting into limp uncertain shapes.
No place so long familiar but it seems
Weird and unwonted in such eery hours.
I wish my taper could have lingered out
Until the yellow dawn.   Was that the wind
Hissing between the jarring lattice crannies,
Or a whispering voice in the room? Hush there again!
Nay 'tis the wind.   What voice should come to me?
I hear no voices, I; no visions yet
Break on my trancèd eyes when I seek God.
I have not risen so high; neither I think
Fallen so at Satan's mercy that he dare
Front me with open tokens of the watch
Which he keeps whensoe'er one of his foes
Keeps holy watch alone.   Yes, there again!

It is the rising wind-gust. How it moves
The shadow of that pine-bough on the wall,
Just growing plain-defined upon the square
The window makes of light across the room.
One might see it like an arm now, finger stretched
In act to curse—a withered witch-like arm
Waving its spells. But then another shadow,
The cross from the mullions, lies athwart it there
And that is steady. So the cross prevails
Over the curse.

    Nay I am idle now
Wasting my vigil time in childish pranks
With unloosed fancy. Though I seem too tired
To school my wayward thoughts it must be done,
They must not wander thus. But this grey glint,
Not light nor darkness, but between, like dreams
When one has slept and struggles to awake,
Unfits one for the real things of thought.
I wonder is the spirit-world more near
In the mystery of twilight than when day
Floods its broad reckless sunlight everywhere.
One *feels* it nearer. In these creeping hours
One might so readily, when one had prayed

With a spiritual passion half the night
To have some message sent one, something shown
That should reveal one clearly chosen His
To glorify Him to the world, be fooled
By eager faith and think that in the dusk
One saw the longed-for vision, or one knew
A voice inborne upon one's soul; while yet
The high revealings were not granted one
Found too unworthy still. Sometimes I think
For me there is that danger—not to-night,
I am so heavy with the weight of sleep
Upon my struggling lips—no not to-night;
I feel too far from God even to be duped
By poor rapt fancy, communing with shadows,
Exulting ignorant in the dread deceit
Which sets in place of God's most marvellous blessing
A mocking and a curse.

      Yet why a curse?
If honour grow to God and nought be falsed
Save something in the powers of one poor mind
That dreams and is the holier and more glad,
What were so much amiss? Why it might be
That God works so upon his messengers,

Not giving them the visions, as they think,
In some true substance, heavenly, made pure
From the earth matter, yet left evident
To eyes and ears; but giving to their souls
A consciousness, nay why not say a dream,
Real because He wills, not in itself,
Having no outward counterpart? And thus—
Sometimes I think it, pondering on the lives
Of some of those most favoured—they might say
" I heard, I saw," and speak Heaven's perfect truth,
And yet be dreamers in the human sense.
Dreamers! and I who fear to dream, and pray
To be saved, as from a lurking enemy,
From my too eager self! But, if 'twere thus
That God revealed Himself, what should one think
Of keeping guard against one's passioned hopes
For fear of self-deceit? Would that be war
Against oneself or God? Why, self deceit
Would be that God deceived one, would be truth
Beyond the truest human yea and nay.
It rather seems one should be effortless,
A leaf upon the river, or a leaf
At the will of the unwarning winds of heaven.

Yes, could one, being in a state of grace,
Grow vacant of all will and merely wait
In a moodless passive lull, what likelier
Than that such were the moment to receive
The glow spiritual, and that the quick tide
Of thoughts and rapt imaginings flooding in
Upon the soul upbreaking from its hush
Were not one's own, but Heaven's? Needs there voice
Heard with the ears, or shape seen with the eyes,
Or aught in contact with the body's sense,
To make the spirit's high realities?
Who knows what visions are? Why should I fear
To think I see and see not? If the Lord
Be pleased to press upon His handmaid's soul
Revealings of His glory, should I urge
Our crude material tests and then "If dreams
Then these were nothings"? But such dreams vouchsafed
Must be—can I err in thinking this?—God's facts,
Beside which all we know by outward proof
Were liker nothings, mere clay images
To evidence to the lower human life
What the divine life in the saint's freed soul
Perceives as souls perceive in Heaven.

And yet

Signs outward have been proved: some have been seen
By the eyes of many, crowned with marvellous light,
Or in their presence lifted from the earth.
There have been visible tokens—was there not
Our own St Catherine who received the wounds
In an awful mystery, bearing them till death?
Or could such be a constant vision pressed
On the eyes of all who looked? Yet scarcely that.

Still she and such as she would need no proofs;
Would *know* when Heaven was open to them—
proofs
Are for bystanders; but when lonely saints
Unwatched, in still communion with their God,
Kneel silently and have forgotten earth,
Need the outward sense bear part in ecstasies
Sent to the soul or—?

What have I to do
With questioning knotty matters hard for me
A babe in the faith? The dawn is mellowing
A little gold into its leaden lights:
My time for retrospect creeps to its end,
And I cannot think, although I know I dreamed

A something of my old life in the night,
That I have met the order given me
To the true fullness. Let me try at least
Somewhat more like confession of the faults
That should be to me in this better state
Each a distinct and hated memory.
But ah! it is so hard to summon them!
Would I were not so weary!

       Fainting star,
Shivering above the strip of presage dawn,
Do you tremble at the glory stealing on
In which the world will lose you presently?
You are like one dying, one who chills and fears
While Heaven is closing round to hide his life,
He knows not how, with God. Why, it is darked:
A little cloud come on it—one might say
Death on it, and that when it issues thence
It will be flooded with the waiting glory
As the saint's soul is.

      So the martyrs passed—
The blackness of an hour of agony,
And then the eternal light, the warmth, the love,
The triumph! Ah the second Catherine,

Whose painful course I keep before my eyes
As one we who live late may still achieve,
Has left a sadder wearier history
Than the first, the Alexandrian saint's. To live
A few short lifeful years made glorious
By the open courage daily fronting death,
By battle in God's name, and victories
On souls fought from false gods, and then to die
In the highest victory God has given His own,
Die His before the eyes of thousands, die
In honour that earth cannot parallel,
Nor Heaven itself surpass, die martyr-crowned,
The glory of the Church to the end of time,
The marvel of the onlooking heathen world!
Yes, that, if in this dull indifferent age
That owns the creed and neither makes nor mars
But lets the saintship grow in the shade and then
Scores it to its own credit, such a life
Could find a place and such a death be earned,
That were the leadership to follow forth
With one's whole will and passion. Not perplexed,
I think, would such a stirring conflict be,
Like that my slow life wages in the dark:

And then the grander ending! Yet the years
Of patient war on sin and the poor flesh,
Of the second Catherine, won her ecstasies
Not less than tranced the other, and at last
She had her meed of honour, and her name
Is all I ought—Oh but I am too fond
In my aspiring when I say so much—
Is more than all I ought to hope for mine
Among names everlasting.

　　　　　　　　　And why not
My name among the holy ones like hers?
Can I not fast and pray, tear my scarred flesh,
Keep vigils day and night, dim my tired eyes
With constant weepings, stint my earthly heart
Of its most innocent food and starve it numb
With ceaseless self-denial, check my life
Even in its holiest vents? What could she more?
And I, weak as I am and prone to faint,
The fever of young life in the free world
So newly passed from me, I do not shrink
From the sharpest discipline. These many months,
Not always fainting, I have schooled myself
Upon her rigorous pattern—God alone

Knows with what strained endurance—and the proofs
Of my hardwon advance are not withheld.
At times I feel my soul borne up to Heaven
In holy rapture and I seem to breathe
A life that is not earth's: at times a hush
Falls on my being and I feel at hand
The Holy Presence, feeling nought beside,
Dulled to all passing round me : and at times
An influence is upon me and the fire
Is kindled in my heart and my words break
Into exultant praises, bursts of love,
Or else in warnings and in passionate pleadings
Torn out with sobbings and with eloquence
That is not mine and urges me myself
Even more than the awed sisters who press round,
Weeping and shaken to the very souls,
And know not what to think of the strange power
That thrills them through and through.   The mother
       says
"'Tis a good gift—let it have vent, my child ;
A blessed gift for bettering your soul
And ours;" but I perceive that secretly
She holds it more than that.   The other day

She said—a speech so venturous for her
That she must long have weighed it—" Daughter, I
    know
That God has work for one like you to do,
Although I know not what: prepare for it:
Be patient, but be ready." And I knew
A reverence in her voice, as though she spoke
To one above her.

             " God has work " she said.
Would it were come! I hunger for my work,
And see none nearer than my coming rule
Over this convent, none more glorious
Than the restricting some small laxities
In the general discipline. A petty task
For which to spur oneself.

             And yet I know not—
To carry such a change as I have planned
To be, as 'twere, through the new saintly practice
The second founder of our sisterhood,
Perhaps of our whole order, were this not
A work to be remembered, work worth me?

   A troubled one perhaps : the better then.
More room for zeal for God, and, overcoming,

More to have overcome.

                       Enough to do.

The mother, pious as she is, falls short

In courage to constrain less pious wills,

And wavers at a tear or a chafed look.

She is content moreover, sees no lapse

In the rigour of our system. 'Twill be mine

To bring the stricter laws, to wake the glow

Of a new zeal among the sisterhood

And fan it into flame, to check the growth

Of such self-sparing in the duller sort

And baby prattlings and small baby joys

In the lighter-natured as we have here now.

They must have longer vigils, sharper fasts,

Be more alone, have many hours for silence

Being together, learn to find their rest,

Their pleasure and their converse all in prayer.

Our novices must have their freedoms clipped;

They are spared too much at first, and spared too

         long;

They need a separate monitress, less lax,

Less pitiful-hearted than the mother is,

Yet loving them no less, one I shall choose

Among those of the sisterhood most true
To the new type, one of the saintly band
Who, gathering round the flame I shall have lit,
Will keep it living and fan on its course
Until it soars a beacon to the world,
A pure accepted altar-fire to Heaven.

    I plan and plan, as if in all the years
That have to run till then there were not time
To fix my.ceaseless purposes in shape,
And look not meanwhile how these minutes lose
The purpose given them and grow too few.
The morning flush has broken on the clouds
While I sat blindly watching, and wanes off:
The shimmering light is broadening into day:
The night is gone—another night laid by
To wait for us in the sepulchre of Time
With his dead children that return no more,
Until they rise in witness on The Day
To show us as we were when they beheld.
The night is gone—and I how have I used it?
Ah me! I think, amiss; but I know not.
I call to mind a night-long wilderment
Of memories and dreams, and some regrets—

I fear me much some semblance of regrets,
And a great penitence. Or am I wrong?
Did I fall asleep and dream the penitence?
For how did I so greatly sin? And yet
I do not think sleep snared me, for my mind
Was all absorbed, and when 'tis thus the body
Is triumphed over. Then I dimly know
Some deep mysterious moments—as if then—
How was it? Nay I have forgotten all;
It is but like recalling waking dreams
After a slumbrous night has dropped on them.

    But this I think, I cannot cross myself
And say "I have performed the allotted task,"
And take the innocent hour of sleep allowed
Before the matin chime. I have not used
The sharp assaying meant, but in the place
Of pitiless self-rebuke and searchings out
Have dreamed, I know not what, a misty world
Of shapeless thoughts that stand like new-made
       ghosts
Between the dead and living. Is there time?
I must redeem the time. Go, tempting sleep:
My rest shall be to earn rest for my conscience.

How the day brightens on!

                 "My ancient life
With all its sins and follies." Well I set
That which for over-long was my all life
First on the roll. "My folly and my sin"
What else, since for so long it darkened Heaven
Out from my tear-blurred sight? But dwelling on it
Even now comes nearer sin than penitence.
Let the poor love-tale go! Oh never more
Let the treacherous memory stir me; it was that
That broke my calm last night and—

                         Let it be,
Oh idle heart! Why wilt thou tempt thyself?
The dead wasp stings lying in the faded rose
When the chills have killed them both—Let the
      wasp rot:
No need to risk a sudden hand to crush it.
Let the rose rot too, though its last breath be sweet,
Let it drop into the hiding mould-heaps dead
With the dead burden that is danger in it.

    And so, the dead love reckoned, what stands
      next?
Ah the long haunting voice that called my sin

Of taking back the life once meant for God
So darkly, deadly, near—that only hope
Called it not quite—the sin against the Spirit!
No, that, the horror of so many months,
Had been the foremost, worst, the all, to reckon,
Hiding all others in its awfulness,
If I still owned it with the strange despair
My uncle's words, denouncing, terrible,
Made my soul's bitter portion once. But now
That dread is past. I was not guilty thus.
I know it, in my inmost heart I know it.
Good Father Andrea—you who, with your gift
Of patient comforting, first lighted me
From that dim horror—you whose pastoral hand
Came, while I seemed to wait and care no more,
Lone on the dead sea of despondency,
And the chill waters lapping round their prey
Bore me indifferent to the shores of Hell,
Came heaven-blessed and stayed me—I know now
With fuller certainty than you could give,
By God's own comforting I think. I look
Clear-eyed upon *that* past. The fault was theirs
Who thought it wise to rate as purposes

6

The fanciful longings of an almost child
Let fall at fluent moments, wise to call
Her natural yearnings for some scope beyond
The round of foolish struttings petty forms,
And petty prides and petty policies
Vocation for a ministry to Heaven.
What knew I of vocation? I was galled
By the bird-snare fetters round me, longed to fly
On wild young wings towards the freer Heaven;
And, seeing that the cage hung on the tree
Was higher than the nest upon the ground,
Said sometimes "Yet at least if I were there,"
Because I so might reach a purer sky
And breathe untainted air; but most of all
Because I longed to soar.

                    An almost child:
Ah yes, how young I was until my love
Awaked me woman. What had I perceived
Of the world's earnest? I could lose myself
In the high rhapsodies of eager youth,
Flame at the wrongs and weakness of the times,
And shudder at the sin; could dream the while
Of heroisms I no more understood

In their plain natures than those names of evils
I hurled my angers at; could hope and plan
Impossible better things and, imaging
A present Paradise of the whole world
If men would only think a few new thoughts,
Talk reasoning unreason, fiery-tongued,
On its blurred good and bad. But what knew I
Of its bad or of its good? My reasonings,
Silent or spoken in unguarded bursts,
What were they but a fluent ignorance
Nursed upon dreams?

            They said, "She is early ripe:
Fifteen, and yet she judges of the world
As one who has all things tried and found them vain
In a grave experience: 'tis a happy thing
That she accepts the convent: we are borne clear:
She accepts it freely, being mature to choose."
And the deep world I thought I weighed and spurned
As wanting in the balance, nevertheless
Had shown me nothing of its meaning yet:
And I had not seen its brightness, had not known
What pleasure meant, when saying "It is naught,"
Nor happiness, when saying "Heaven's is all;"

                6—2

And had not known the triumphs of sweet praise
On the general tongue and ringing to the ears
Of one dear over all, and had not known
The gladness of dear hope, and had not known,
Had not conceived, what love was, love-sought love,
When saying " Life is weary every day
And the wide world is barren to the heart. "
They were too prompt to take my girlish fits
Of dream enthusiasm for the dream I made
Of an ideal perfectness withdrawn
From reach of sin and sorrow in the hush
Of convent calm, and turn them to their will.
The fault was theirs. But I, knowing my God
Hears me and judges, say I never framed
A set intention, spoke one purposed word
Pledging me to the life I ranked so high.
'Tis doubtless true, as Father Andrea says,
That my accuser bore me in his heart
Guiltless of that great blame and did but think
To daunt me to submission by a dread
So horrible. " Yes, yes, believe me, daughter,"
The good man always said, "'tis as I told you :
His Eminence spoke from prudence, seeing there

A way to scare you to your good, no more;
Take this for proof—only you must not know
How it came to me—he said, even on the day
You took the vows, it would have pleased him more
If you, instead of flaunting girlish scorn
At a certain great alliance hinted yours
If you so pleased, had let it be your choice
Before the convent."

            So I take the proof.
It fits with what his dullard Princeliness—
When he deigned to think that I, although less fair
Than the sister he had bought, might please his moods
With a more apt variety and reward
His condescending choice by more applause
For how his princess played her brilliant part,
And, nothing doubting my delight, with mouths
Of secrecy and eyes significant,
Blinking owl mystery, and "Trust to me"
And "Never fear I'll bring the matter through"
Confided me his project—seemed to assure
As if he had tried his way, "No convent, no;
This queenly Eva must not hide from us;
She is to shine in the world. Let her but smile

And put a little hand in mine; I promise
That from that moment none shall frighten her
With the hateful veil." And when indignantly
I turned on him "And the betrothal, sir,
Already fixed with Leonora, that
Is a mere mock it seems, a promise given
To come for an hour of pastime one fair day
That may be broken for some light excuse,
Some merrier fooling coming in the way!
What pretty trifle have you on your tongue
To turn it daintily as a courtier should
To our mother and my uncle?" He laughed low.
"Leave it to me, child. They are my good friends,
And Leonora has a lovely face,
And, were she sister to my wife, might have
A pretty dower. Ask if they're content
When I have told them you are." Add to that
A hundred trifles not detected then
In their joint significance, which now summed up
Make evidence—well, for them or against?
Which shall I say? What matters it to me,
Except to show that torturing charge, tricked out
A bugbear for my conscience, meant no more

Than the noises nurses make behind the wall
To frighten children quiet in their beds?
So let that pass, it need not swell the score.
But other sins? the many, what of them?
No easy reckoning this. Too well I know
My youth was girlish-wayward, too well know
My heart fed too much on the things of earth :
I know that many follies, many faults,
Had scarred that early life that seems so like
An innocence in looking back on it :
But how to say " In this and this I sinned—
Here evil dashed the good—there all was evil,"
Seems as if, coming from a woodland path,
One should essay to chronicle the thorns
Set on the briar rose-trees, count the size
And order of the flint-stones by the way
Upon the moss-banks and the grassy rims.
They were there, one saw them, one remembers that,
But one thinks more of the roses.

     Well but pride,
My sin of pride—which we of our old house,
Following its long traditions, arrogate
A prerogative to ourselves, a loyalty

Done to our race—my sin that most to me
Seemed virtue-like, that grasped so deep a part
Of my natural life that its mere name pronounced
Stands for a thousand separate confessions—
Let it take its fitting place, and be my shame
That was my ill-placed glory. Poor fond fool
To plume myself on having missed the grace
Of Heaven's high humility! and then
He made the fault so dear, he, when he said
He loved me for it—that still summer-day
When first was spoken what we knew so well
For long before, when a too welcome chance
Had lost us from the others laughing on
Along the olive slopes, and we two found
The boat upon the little silent lake
Left all alone, and stole it from its place,
And let it drift into the happy shade
Beneath the bank where the acacias pushed
Their boles into the water through the trails
Of creeping briony and red roses drooped
Lush sprays above my head. He said it then
When I, in the childishness of happy love,
Had whispered on his breast that question old

And meaningless as the song the linnet sings,
The question that glad lovers love to ask
And answer and hear answered: " Tell me, love,
What made you love me first?" "Perhaps it was,
My own proud Eva, that same queenly pride
Which, jesting, I have blamed you for, that pride
Which keeps you nobler-lived than other women."
"My own proud Eva," that was how he called me
In many a stolen whisper afterwards:
"My own proud darling"—and my idle heart
Was ever beating to the pleasant rhythm,
And I loved my pride because he loved it in me.
Oh! many and many sullen self-despites
And frettings at myself and weary moods
Of half-revolt and utter hopelessness,
When even penitence was tired away
And I was only angry, since have paid
The forfeit of those self-deceiving days;
And I have felt my closest being wrung
By the very chains I heaped on it myself
To bow it to the need; and I have striven
In twofold anguish, torn in my racked mind
Between the natural and the new-learned will;

And I have sickened at very victory
Loathing my lowliness. Ah me! those days
How long they were! how cruel! But, I thank
The grace of Heaven for it, I endured,
I overcame. My pride is crushed at length
Into the dust that fits it, and my foot
Presses its writhing neck; never again
Shall it rise up to chafe and weary me
With the old onslaughts.

　　　　　　　　　　Pride, yes; and, pride confessed,
One has confessed a humour over apt
To sudden scorns and high-flown discontents
And the petulance of disdain. But anger's self,
A deadly sin, is nothing more than these;
And there too am I guilty.

　　　　　　　　　　　　Little bird,
Flitting so daintily upon the sill,
Hast thou come to tell me with thy matin chirp
That all the day-world is astir? I know,
But I am fettered to my drowsy thoughts;
I cannot gladden to the sun like thee.
Chirp, chirp, how glad thou art. Do the dull nights
Seem long now in these autumn times? But then,

Birdie, thy days are never over long.
We cannot say so much, we the world's lords:
Often the weary never-ending days
Burden us helpless with their dragging weight.
Thou art happier than thou knowest—all the more
Because thou dost not know that thou art happy.
We never wear our happiness so light,
Always oppressed by our strong consciousness
Whose deeps lie so near pain.
                    Already gone?
Yes, fly, wee wanderer, back to thy blithe grove
Warm with the earliest sunshine mellowing
The curves of spreading tree-tops. Out of sight
So soon?—no, on that cypress.
                    What do I
Watching the idle rovings of a bird,
With vacant purpose?
                 I have thought too long,
I lose myself. What wonder? In one night
To live back all one's youth—though mine was short.
And yet it seems a long long age of life
Remote by longer ages. Strange it is
That the brief exquisite mood of a deep bliss

Which, being lived, seemed to be some few hours,
Seems, being lost, as if a long life's whole
Had passed in it. 'Twas but a year or so,
Count it by days upon the calendar,
And now—

        Oh living days! oh happy days!
Oh days adream with happiness!—adream—
Adream—I am with you—Ah yes—adream
I am with you

    *   *   *   *   *   *   *

        What was I pondering
Before this drowsy languor stole my will?
Let me remember.

        Yes the sins and follies
Of my vain youth. But I had almost done—
Or had I? Where was I in the blurred page
Whose half-forgotten fragment-facts from days
That were no more all faults than all good deeds
I am bidden read in the dusk that time has made?
Ah me! how to bethink me? When there grows
The counterfeit of some large landscape known
In past familiar days upon that sense
Which seems an inward memory of the eye—

Grows, at the plainest even, half as if
One looked upon it with the former sight—
If one were bidden break the vivid whole
Into its several parts traced point by point,
Or more, if one were bidden duly note
The rocks that broke the smoothness of the lake,
Or the black fissures on the great snow-hills,
Or say the pools along the marshy wastes,
How the thought-picture would become perplexed
Into a shifting puzzle, and the sight
Would ache that vainly tried to scan by units.
Even so it seems to me when I essay
To singly look upon the marring flaws
That foiled my youth's best virtues, or on those
That of its evil made the blackest scars.

    Weary, so weary of the effort! Nay
I *will* remember! Well, my girlish days
Were full of faults—were doubtless full of faults—
Were full of faults: but what were the faults' names?
I am forgetting what I seek—their names?
Why there was many a paltry selfishness—
Many no doubt, for I was often shamed
To be so much below the self I dreamed—

Only I cannot call them singly back.
And there were pettish quarrels, girlish-wise,
With one or other of the rest at home,
Oftenest with Leonora, though, I think,
We chose each other most, and she has kept
My memory dearest of them; she alone
Remembers my old name-day, comes to me,
As if it still were festival to me,
With flowers, and calls me Eva.

                             Does she guess,
I wonder, that I could have stolen her greatness?
Poor Leonora, would she have lost much?
Wife's sister to the prince instead of wife;
That dowry he designed her for amends,
To make her welcome to some simpler home—
Perhaps with love with it, such as *we* hoped
When we were lovers—Yes, perhaps with some one
Who could have taught her smiles: she only laughs.
I would I knew her happy now! She says
She is most happy: but she says she knows
Nothing worth sorrow.

                        Nothing! Nothing worth
The weeping out one's life for! Nothing worth

The wearying after in a waking dream
Of all one's days, the straining to one's heart
As a mother her one child, her one dead child,
Although a plague had stricken it and the end
Were her own dying! Nothing worth a sorrow
Dearer than any future joy could be,
Stronger than love, oh! longer lived than love,
Than love itself, a sorrow to be lived for
Liked love itself, to be one's closest life!
If only one were free to sorrow thus!
Oh to be left my sorrow for a while,
Only a little while! to weep at will!
Oh let me weep a while if but for shame
Because I cannot check the foolish passion,
Because I weep despite myself. Alas!
Oh Lord my helper, when shall I find rest?

  * * * * *

How sweet those roses smell! Look, Angelo,
That cluster of red roses pictured back
From the still water. See! see! Catch that branch
By your left hand—the boat will drift away!
How the boat rocks! how it rocks! Am I ashore?
I thought I was in the boat with you. How it rocks!

Oh Angelo !

   What is it? Where am I?
Who was it screamed? Was it I?

      I have been dreaming—
How plain it was at first! We in the boat
On the still lake, just as we were that day,
The roses drooping on us, and, far spread
On the clear water, greenness of the trees.
A strangely real dream! And then the change——
The tossing waters, I ashore alone
Watching—and then—oh! that white anguished face
Uplifting from the waters as they heaved
About him sinking!

    Whence came such a dream?
He is with Giulia happy. I ——

       Am here
Vowed to the convent, vowed to Heaven's service,
And happy in the faith of Heaven's reward.
I have not quite forgotten Whose I am,
And in the waking day can call to mind
What higher lot is mine and be in it
In peace.

    But yet I would I had not seen

That haggard face.   I fear me many days
Will find it haunting me.   It was too like
The look he gave me when our eyes last met,
When all was over, and there was for us
No farewell but that sudden chance-caught look
In a busy street, and then we had passed on.

    The chapel bell at last.   Never its sound
Has fallen kinder on my ear.   Now comes
The rest of prayer; and so the day begins
Its round of holy duties, and my strength
Will grow again towards them.   It will pass,
This querulous weakness with my weariness—
It *has* passed; I am strong; I am myself;
My God did but forsake me for a while.
He hears, He calls me to Him at the shrine.
He will forgive me, me whom He has chosen;
He will fold me in His love.   Am I not His?

    But yet I would I had not seen that face.

SISTER ANNUNCIATA.

II. ABBESS URSULA'S LECTURE.

My daughter, do you guess why I chose you
As my to-day's companion for the hour
I warm me in the winter sunshine here,
Sitting where many sleep whom I have known
My new-come novices like your young self?
I am an old woman now, sadly infirm,
My senses failing, but I sometimes catch
A whisper never meant to reach my ear.
I heard yours yesterday. You "think it strange
That I should choose to haunt the burial ground
Alive : 'twere time enough when I am dead."
A careless speech, dear child : if you had thought,
You would have phrased your wonder differently.
But I will answer it. So many years
I have been old that it is out of mind
How long I have been face to face with death :
And by God's mercy I have long lost fear.
None of us should fear death : a nun's true life

Begins in Heaven; you should remember this.
But I have custom to my aid; at nights
When I lie down I think "It may be sleep
Or may be death," and close my eyes in calm;
And when the sun falls warmest in the day
I have myself brought here, and often think
How soon I shall be here asleep in Christ,
And do not find it an unhappy thought.
And there are more companions here for me
Than in the convent. For I am so old
That there is no one in the convent now
Who saw me come, excepting sister Clare,
And she bedridden. Yes, no doubt, my child,
I have outlived my life and seem to youth
A sort of ghost already—just a ghost
From old old days, and so I haunt the place
Where many like me rise to be with me:
I feel them near me here. Poor child, you shrink.
Nay, if the blessed spirits really came
In presence near us, it were cause for joy:
I'd have you long for such revealings given
From the higher world. But I meant not so much;
Only the thoughts of them and memories

7—2

That seem to reach me from these quiet graves.
There are graves there from which, had I more
    strength,
I could read you many histories which, perhaps,
Might move you more to what I fain would teach
Than I can do.

           See, there is one. Look left,
The corner grave beneath the sycamore,
That with the cross a little fallen slant.
There sleeps the saintliest creature! had she lived
The Church would surely have enrolled her name
Upon its calendar. She was to be
Abbess here after me, so was it planned,
And often I felt shamed to think how far
My fervent-souled successor would surpass
My poor endeavours for the convent's good,
And how more far surpass them in the life
Set for a pattern to the younger nuns.
But she was more than holy-lived; on her
Came wondrous power from heaven, we knew not
    what,
If inspiration or mere eloquence
Moved by a fervour strange to common souls.

Myself and many others have at times,
Feeling strange influence working in our hearts
While she, the rapture on her, spoke and spoke
And took authority on her, believed
She was a chosen messenger of God,
And almost looked to see some miracle
Declare her to us. She had visions too,
But these came later: she was near her end
When they began; but that we did not know.
She died one summer—well, well, I forget
How many years ago—before your birth.
Yes, on a summer evening I know,
For the sunset light came full into her room,
And 'twas the one next mine. She died one sum-
          mer;
And some months earlier, at this time of year
But on a day most different from this,
All rain and chill and dreariness, they came
And woke me in the morning, telling me
Sister Annunciata had been found
Stretched in a swoon, and now so long remained
Rigid and speechless that death must be near.
She had had a vision then, the first she had;

She told me of it with her first faint words
As she recovered. Some one came, she said,
Who had been dear to her, and, whispering close
Beside her bed where she lay taking sleep
After a half-night's vigil, tempted her
To pray to heaven that heaven might be for her
Eternal life with one she once had loved—
Whether the same who spoke I gathered not;
She said "Ah! make me not remember now
Whom the saints' selves have bidden me forget,"
When I asked her of that matter. Well, she said,
While she was struggling in a sort of maze
Between a wish to shriek the prayer aloud
And a half-sense of something more than her
That checked it, and the voice was making moan
"Oh Eva do not lose us our last hope,"
She heard a cry that clanged out like the burst
Of treble organ pipes when the high strains
Take up the Gloria in our Easter mass,
"Annunciata wake, wake." Starting up,
Still sobbing, as she said, she knew a dream
Had troubled her: but there stood, where the light
That trembled dimly from the cloud-barred moon

In a gap of sky just fell upon the folds
Of their white raiment, two pale shimmering forms
Whose faces at the first she did not see.
And, when assured they were not also dreams
Or fancies of her fevered eyes and brain
In the sudden waking, she believed them Angels.
But when one spoke she knew—though by what sign
She could not tell me that first time—they were
St Catherine of Alexandria
And our St Catherine of Sienna, each
Holding the other's hand. Which spoke the words
She knew not—Afterwards she grew to mark
Her visions more distinctly; that first time
She was amazed and troubled. These the words:
"We have rescued thee, but henceforth take thou heed
Lest thou be left to struggle by thyself
And fall. Thy heart unfaithful to thy Lord
Remembers, and God says to thee 'Forget.'"
And then they made as if they would have gone,
Yet turned to her again and said "Approach
And feel our presence, that thou mayest be sure
We have been with thee." But, as she advanced,
A terror came upon her, and she fell,

And knew no more.

            Thenceforward oftentimes
She had most wondrous visions: holy saints
Appeared to her, oftenest of all those two
Whom she saw first, and heavenly harmonies
Waked her of nights, and voices spake to her.
And every day we saw her saintlier,
And felt her growing more apart from us,
As one marked out for deeper purposes
Than we could fathom. Yet she still remained
Humble among us; always she preferred
The lowest offices, and eagerly
Abased herself, "I have been proud," she said,
"And even proud of pride; my penitence
Is to be meaner than the meanest here."

    Ah well! you may believe that none of us
Would so account her. Though I kept her down
To the rule of strict obedience like the rest,
Believe me that, but for the honour due
Unto my office, I perceived myself
So poor beside her, so unworthy even
To kiss her garment's hem, I could have knelt
And cried "Oh saint, take rule upon us all

And let me be thy servant;" but I knew
What duty my high office laid on me.

    But think of her, proud as she well might be—
She came of the Albizzi—young as you,
Renowned already for the liveliest wit
And wisest, after woman's sort, then found
Among the brightest ladyhood of Rome,
Talked of for beauty too. She, with so much
Already tasted of earth's sweetest cup,
And so much more yet brimming to her lips
At the moment 'twas withdrawn, gave up her life
So wholly unto Heaven that, still on earth,
She seemed to see the brightness of God's face,
And was as if bedazzled by the light
Blind to all lower things; and so to her
It was as if in earth was only heaven.

    How plain I see her dying! You may know
She died in happiness. Through several months
She saw the visions, they came oftener
And oftener, until, towards the last,
She saw them nightly. Sometimes too they came
In the broad daylight, when she would be lost,
As she was often, in her prayers alone

In the silent chapel. When the summer grew
Towards its fall they left her utterly,
And she, already paler than you see
St Barbara in the picture in the choir
And looking nearer death, she drooped at this,
Stricken with anguish; for she read in it
A sign of wrath divine against some fault
Her holy soul discerned in the perfectness
Of a most singularly holy life.
So the blow fell on her, and she soon knew—
The first of us she knew, and silently—
That she was dying. Then—she knew not why,
For the voices never came again—she felt
That she was once more in the grace of God,
And a great peace fell on her. This she told
When she sent for me on the day when first
She did not rise at dawn but quietly
Lay on her bed and said "Death is at hand."
Three days we watched her weakening. All the while
We seldom heard her speak; she lay asleep,
Or wept or smiled half-sleeping. On the fourth
She roused and thanked me—thanked us all for care
And watchings in her illness—me besides

For some old kindness, something said or done,
I could not rightly gather what she meant,
At the time of her first coming. This I know,
Her thankfulness, so long kept in her heart,
Uttered at such a moment, dwells in me
A lesson for my guiding, and I hope
That I have seldomer failed in gentleness
And a mother's sympathy for the young souls
New to our holy bondage who, may be,
Are sad and restless for a little while.

    I said to her "My daughter, I was blessed,
Beyond my knowing, when a word of mine
Was sown to such ripe fruit in you." Her eyes
Looked earnest at me "Mothers smile like you";
And that was all. She spoke not much again,
Nor aught to be remembered, but, till day
Was passing into sunset she was with us,
Lying so still we scarcely could discern
Whether she waked or slept. The sunlight fell
Right on her bed at evening, and I thought
The yellow beams too strong upon her eyes;
I moved to shade them, then she took my hand,
Just touched it faintly, for her strength was gone,

"Such happy rest" she said, "God's rest" and smiled,
Then fell asleep. And presently one said
"She is dead," and then another "She is dead,"
And we perceived she was no more with us,
Although the smile was strengthening on her face.

Some thought it was a wonder nothing strange
Was noticed at her death-bed; none of us
Would have thought it any wonder had there been
Tokens from Heaven plainly granted her
Before us all, and she had been shewn forth
As one whose name was henceforth to be famed
With more than human honour. But God's will
Was not to crown our humble convent here
With such a glory.

           When she was laid out,
I took my niece's baby secretly
To touch the body, thinking that, perchance,
There might be virtue in it, by God's grace
And with our many prayers for the poor child,
To give its poor blind eyes their sight. Poor child,
It was not so to be.

           Now will you learn
A hope from that most holy life? Well, she

Who was as I have told you, had at first
A restless heart and angry at restraint,
And looked, as you may do, with wistful eyes,
Back to the world behind. I know not why—
She came of her free-will, even like myself
Who loved the quiet of the convent best
Quite from the first—and like you too, you say,
Who do not love it yet, I think. She might,
Had she so chosen, have become the wife
Of one whose wealth and greatness were the theme
Of all the gossipries of Rome: but she
Came here and brought her proud and wayward
      heart
To fret and chafe at her imprisonment
For many days. I have told you of the end:
Do you not think it worth your envying?
And who can say 'tis not within your reach?
But be persuaded, at the least, of this,
That you may learn her joy in heavenly things,
And know at last even such a peace in death.

THE SNOW WASTE.

WITH THE DEAD.

THE SNOW WASTE.

I saw one sitting mid a waste of snow
Where never sun looked down nor silvering moon,
But far around the silent skies were grey,
With chill far stars bespeckled here and there,
And a great stillness brooded over all.
And nought was there that broke the level plain,
And nothing living was there but himself.
Yet was he not alone, there stood by him
One right, one left, two forms that seemed of flesh,
But blue with the first clutchings of their deaths,
Fixed rigid in the death-pang, glassy-eyed,
Turning towards him each a vacant gaze.
And he looked on them blankly, turn by turn,
With gaze as void as theirs. He uttered speech

8

That was as though his voice spoke of itself
And swayed by no part of the life in him,
In an uncadenced chant on one slow chord
Dull undulating surely to and fro.
And thus it ran.

"Ye dead who comrade me amid this snow
Where through long æons I drag me to and fro,
I speak again to ye the things I know
But, knowing, cannot feel, that haply so
I may relight in me life's former glow
And thaw the ice-bound tears in me to flow,
If I might into sentient memory grow
And waken in me energy of woe.

"For there is left in me full memory
Of things that were to me in days gone by,
And I can read them with my inward eye;
But like a book whose fair-writ phrases lie
All shapely moulded to word-harmony
But void of meaning in their melody,
Vague echoes that awaken no reply
In my laxed mind that knows not what they cry.

"And I can reason duly with my thought,
And am not lessened of its range in aught,
Can reckon all the deeds that I have wrought
And say, 'Here lurked the canker taint that brought
The plague whereby thy whole man was distraught,
Here with a grace of good the act was fraught,
A dew of love here slaked the desert drought,
Thy sin in truth hath here the vengeance brought.'

"So can I reckoning keep of woe and weal,
And mine own self unto myself reveal
In perfect knowledge : but I cannot feel.
And all the past across my mind will steal
And leave as little trace as the swift keel
Upon the lake's cleft waves that seamless heal :
Cold memory can with the old things but deal
As with the creatures of some show unreal.

"I know that I was bent beneath the weight
Of wearying sorrow, or grew wroth with fate,
Or was with triumphing and joy elate,
Or bore towards another love or hate,

And ask, 'What were these that had power so great,
These senses in me in my former state?'
And mouth their names out in my hollow prate
To rouse with them my heart inanimate.

"Because I know if I one pang could make
Of sorrow in me, if my heart could ache
One moment for the memories I spake,
The spell that is upon me now might break,
And I might with a sudden anguish shake
The numbness from it and perceive it wake,
And these be no more bound here for my sake
But slumber calmly in their silent lake.

"Then I like other men might pass away,
And cold could no more gnaw me when I lay
Amid these snows a painless heap of clay,
And, though the sharp-tongued frosts my skin
          should flay,
I should not feel, no chills on me could prey
And gnaw their teeth into my bones for aye,
As now is my long doom that will not slay:
I should know no dull torture in decay.

"Ye dead who follow me, I think that ye,
If ye have any being save in me,
Must have much longing that such end should be
To my long wandering, that ye may flee
To the deep grave I gave ye and be free
From bondage here, and in death quiet be,
If ye can know and loathe the bitter lee
Ye drink from my dregged cup by That decree.

"Yet hear, if ye can hear, if ye have might,
Ye dead, to wake my heart from its strange night,
Hear now and waken it while I recite
That which hath brought on it this icy blight,
So I may come to mean my words aright
And not, as now, like some dull purblind wight
Prating by rote of shadow and of light,
Or like an idiot echoing wisdoms trite.

"What love is now I know not; but I know
I once loved much, and then there was no snow.
A woman was with me whose voice was low
With trembling sweetness in my ears, as though

Some part of her on me she did bestow
In only speaking, that made new life flow
Quick through me : yet remembering cannot throw
That spell upon me now from long ago.

" I only know it was, forgetting how,
Nor can remind me why my soul should bow
Before her beauty, nor can gather now
What charm her nobleness of eye and brow
Had with such queenship o'er me to endow ;
My memory can keep count of look and vow
But nothing of their spirit re-allow.
I know, dead woman, that my love art thou.

" I look on thee and him with equal mind.
I know him too : some years my heart was twined
In love round his. He was of noble kind,
He had no rival, leaving all behind ;
Me too he passed, and then my love declined.
But when I knew him first the boy would wind
His younger arms round me, and I would find
Pride in his triumphs next to mine assigned.

"He grew in strength and in all daring fast
Until, as if a sudden chill north blast
Had found me sleeping in the sun, aghast
I woke and knew my glory overcast.
No feat or skill in which I all had passed
But he passed me.   My triumphs had been glassed
In eyes of all the fairest and I classed
First and alone; now I to him was last.

"In all ways last: he was more deft, more gay,
More comely, apter in the minstrel lay;
The brightness of my life had passed away:
I heard his praises echoed day by day:
And she, from whom no thought of mine could stray,
Set all her pride on him: I heard her say
Amid the maidens, 'None, seek where ye may
Will match my brother till his hair is grey.'

"When she was wed to me I sought in vain
By hid degrees her love from him to gain;
It only seemed to move in her such pain
That need was on my hatred to refrain

From open showing of its bitter strain,
Albeit if thought could slay he had been slain,
He nothing doubting. So did all remain
Until the corn was yellow on the plain.

"And even mother earth had loved him more
Than me ; his wide sun-flooded meadows bore
A golden host that numbered mine thrice o'er ;
His vines a richer bloom of promise wore ;
The very river turned it from my shore
That, plenty bringing, it had marged of yore,
To make his pastures richer. Wroth and sore
My heart grew in me, burning at its core.

"Before our door, beneath the palm-tree wide,
One eve I sat alone with my young bride,
For he, who mostly then was by our side,
Some days had gone beyond the lake's far tide
Where the great city basked her in her pride,
And, thinking of him, she was absent-eyed,
And ever in our dearest talk she sighed
'Great God and Light my brother's journey guide.'

"Because a pilgrim had passed by that day
And told us that the golden city lay
Beneath a ghastly plague's devouring sway,
The living could not hide their dead away,
They writhed in human heaps of foul decay,
The glutted vultures lingered o'er their prey
Along the marts, poor fools with minds astray
Howled blasphemies or leaped in ghastly play.

"And loathsome taint, he said, lurked in the air
For miles around, and whoso harboured there
Must look no more to life, unless he were
Even to miracle the Heaven's care.
So, while we watched the red lake's sunset glare,
I only joyed that he might in that snare
Be caught and die: but she could only spare
Half thoughts for me, and sighed for him some
            prayer.

"I knew that there was gladness in my eyes,
But hers were clouded with sad reveries:
I spoke to her of our fair destinies,
She told her fears for him in low replies:

'Yes love him still, still me for him despise,'
I cried, 'What wife have I unless he dies?
Would that he might.' In startled sad surprise
She answered, weeping out a voice of sighs."

But a clear solemn voice rose over his,
" *Thou* speak it." And I saw a lucent form,
As of a spirit making to itself
A pure white brightness, drooping over him
Towards that shape of a dead woman, cry:
" *Thou*, speak it, if so any ghost of love
Might yearn in him towards thee." Her dead lips
Moved not, nor moaned with any breath of words,
Nor passed there any stir across her face,
But a sweet plaining voice came out from her,
A voice as of one weeping at the heart.
" Do I not love thee first and most, my own?
And art thou bitter that my heart has room
For him, my brother? Dost thou chide the sun,
Our light of life and soul, that he will shine
His brightest on him even as on thee?
Wilt thou chide love that is our second light
Because it shines upon him from my heart

Only a little less than upon thee?"
Sadly the voice died off. He, vacantly,
As though he knew her not, met her dead eyes,
.Then with his old unpassioned utterance spoke.

"These were her words and thus did her voice sigh;
Mine hurried from me in a fierce reply
That burst from out my lips with sudden cry,
As though itself had willed to speak, not I,
My secret thought: I wished all love might die
If else he in her love must press me nigh:
Since he must bless my foe, the sun on high
Might dwindle into darkness utterly."

There cried a voice, "Speak thou his very words
That he may hear them spoken as he spoke,
Hear his words, laden with his hateful doom,
In thy voice that he hated: so some ghost
Of passion might awaken in his soul.
Speak *thou* the words." And I saw stand by him
A form of darkness, like a tempest-cloud,
Waving towards that shape of a dead man
That he should speak. And voice came from that
　　　dead,

As from the woman, moving not the lips
Not waking any life in the glazed eyes,
"Thus didst thou say, 'Rather might all love die
Out from the earth for ever than warm *him!*
Rather might all love perish from my life
Than have him wound into thy love with me!
And I *do* hate the sun though he be God.
What love or thanking need I to this God,
Since he but makes me one amid the all?
I curse him. Would that all his vaunted light
Were utter darkness, rather than that he
Alike with me should shine on him I hate!'"

So the voice ceased in tempest. But he looked
One moment on that corpse's livid face
With a dull dreamy loathing in his eyes,
And in the moment they were cold again
With the old quiet nothingness of gaze,
And he spoke on again in shadeless rhythm.

"These were the words wherein I did invoke
Thy doom upon me, naming even the stroke
Of this long vengeance. It was his voice spoke
Thy words again. If for the moment woke
An impulse in my breast to burst its yoke

And leap out through the clogging frosts that choke
Its well-springs, it but seemed as if they broke;
Still do those frosts my stagnant life-blood cloke."

Then the dark shadow cried, "Lo I have failed.
I cannot wake him even by his hate;
He is not given me but bears such doom
As was awarded him by his own words."
And the fair brightness cried, "And I have failed
And he, alas! is left to his dread doom."
And both passed out from him; who still spoke on.
  "And while my words yet on the echoes played,
  The clouds that singly through the blueness strayed,
  Hurled into one a sudden darkness made;
  A shrilling whirlwind all the palm-tops swayed,
  Then stillness. Horror on our spirits weighed,
  And I stood awe-struck, while she knelt and prayed.
  Then through the dark we heard, and were afraid,
  A slow voice speak the doom upon me laid."

Called then a voice that was as though it dropped
From the far stars and rose from the deep snows,
And was in all and over all at once:

" Hear once again: this was the doom pronounced :
' Because thou hast cursed love which is a life
And is God's greatest gift to souls on earth,
All love shall die from thee ; thou shalt not know it
Even in thought. And, since thou hast blasphemed
That which is God to thee, and cursed the day,
Thou shalt have lost all part in day. And know
That herein lies a curse more than thy mind
Can fathom yet. Yet this of hope is given,
Thou hast until to-morrow's sun be sunk
For penitence : so may this less doom be,
To live thy life alone in heart and blind
But yet to die at last as all men die.' "
He listened calmly, and again spoke on.

"One came at noon and told that he to flee
The plague had turned him homewards and would be
Once more with us before the great lake sea
Was flushed to the red evening skies. Then she,
I saw it, in her joy lost thought of me
And could forget a moment That decree.
I went, unwatched to set my passion free;
Perhaps, I thought, unwatched my weird to dree.

"I turned me home at noon.   The house seemed
    lone,
No greeting voice made answer to my own,
But through the hush I heard a frequent moan.
I traced it where I found her anguish-prone,
Her writhing length athwart the cushions thrown,
So left to die, for all in dread had flown :
The black plague-roses on her cheek had blown.
I knew my weird's first working on her shown.

"I did not fear the plague, who inly knew
The doom that had been meted out my due
Must fence me from it though all else it slew :
I held her till the death-films came to glue
Her swollen lids apart : my cold hand drew
Them o'er her faded eye's dull glazing blue :
I still watched by her while the first plague hue
Upon the corpse's face a blackness grew.

"It was at the first evening hour she died ;
And I, so waiting by my dead one's side,
Thought angrily of him who homewards hied,
And joyed that now at least the linkings tied

Between us since his sister was my bride,
Now she was dead were snapt asunder wide.
At length I heard his voice without that cried,
And I went forth and smilingly replied.

"I said, 'Go in, thy sister was distressed,
Long waiting for thee, and I bade her rest:
I think e'en now her eyes are slumber-pressed:
But thou, go clasp the sleeper to thy breast,
Let her be wakened by her looked-for guest:
She said not seeing thee she slept unblest,
And named thee last half-dreaming; do her hest,
Obey the call; 'twill be a goodly jest.

"I led him to her softly: his fresh eye
Could only glimmering outline yet descry,
He saw her silent in the dimness lie,
And breathed, 'Yes she is sleeping,' then drew nigh.
And then I fled, and, that he should not fly,
I fenced the door. And then I watched the sky
That I might count how well the time went by,
And thought, 'He surely will go mad or die.'

"Two hours, then near an hour, passed onward
    slow,
The high east clouds were losing their last glow,
So late it grew, when I returned to know
If any evil came upon my foe.
I only heard a gasping thick and low,
I raised my torch his darkening face to show;
He lay, plague-smitten, in the passing throe.
I mocked him, watching, 'Is the jest but so?'

"He lay beside her, and I could not bear,
Through my great hatred, that he should rest
      there:
Ere yet the life had passed I sought to tear
His arms from her. But suddenly from where
The sun was sleeping, rose an awful glare
That reddened on us. When it ceased to flare
Its fiery anger I had lost all care
Of love or hatred, and I left the pair.

"But, when I was made strong with food and
    wine,
I called to mind that need was to consign

9

The darkening mass to fitter couch than mine,
And could not chose but his close grasp untwine,
That I might drag each where the mountain's
    spine
Broke sudden lakewards in one high-ridged line.
I hurled them downwards. From the steep incline
I watched the startled ripples whirl and dwine.

"And I was calmer than the lake; no throe
Had stirred in me, no eddying of woe;
And when once more it lay unmoved below
I went in peace my tired limbs to bestow
On my freed couch, alone but pangless so,
And slept such quiet sleep as children know:
But I awakened in this waste of snow
Where evermore gnawed by quick cold I go."

He ceased, and looked long with alternate gaze
On the dead faces that were fixed on him,
As seeking in some change in them to read
His change, if any change might grow to him.
But they and he looked still one rigid void.
And nothing stirred along the boundless snows,

And nothing broke the wide unbreathing calm.
He rose, and moved with slow and even pace:
And those strange dead were borne along with him,
As though they were himself. So they passed on.
And far away along the dreadful waste
I heard the droning murmur of his words
But knew not what they bore. And when they died
In distance all things slept in one great hush,
The plain of snow and the unchanging sky.

WITH THE DEAD.

"Has any one ever been lost here?" asked Kenyon of the guide.

*"Surely, signor: one, no longer ago than my father's time,"
said the guide; and he added, with the air of a man who believed
what he was telling, "but the first that went astray here was a pa-
gan of old Rome, who hid himself in order to spy out and betray
the blessed saints, who then dwelt and worshipped in these dismal
places. You have heard the story, signor? A miracle was wrought
upon the accursed one; and, ever since (for fifteen centuries at
least), he has been groping in the darkness, seeking his way out of
the catacomb."*

HAWTHORN'S *Transformation,* Vol. I. ch. 3.

HE hour has come, my hour of yearly rest
From the long madness while I grope my
way
With eager hands through these black clueless vaults,

For ever tracking my unceasing steps
To the same sharp angles and the same low niches,
From day to night not knowing day from night,
Through day and night, not knowing any rest,
Not knowing any thought save that slow horror,
That breathless agony of hope more keen
With hopeless pangs than utter hopelessness,
Not knowing that I am, not knowing aught
Save that I wander, chill with creeping dread,
Seeking in vain through darkness big with death
An egress into life, while my worn limbs
Shiver with terror and my palsied lips
Tremble too much to call upon the gods.

    And now I rest! A dreadful rest, accursed,
Made weary with despair and furious
With the old hate and the old bitter love:
Because I must, despite myself, remember.
Oh me! this added curse of memory
That burns like hissing iron through my soul,
This deadliest undying memory!
And I undying! Heavens; is there no taunt
No curse so loathsome to this angered Power
Who holds me here, that I might hurl it at him

And rouse such flame of wrath as must perforce
Smite me to ashes with its shrivelling breath?
Oh! but to cease to be! to cease to know!
My throat is choked; I writhe in agonies,
Fierce agonies of thought; my life and soul
Are all one pain—Oh! but to cease to know!

I rave in vain. For who should hear me here,
One live among the dead, who shriek for aid
Out from this darkness where the gods look not?

To cease to know? yea, I shall cease to know
In a little while. The blood chills at my heart,
And I grow faint and shudder at the foretaste—
In a little while! and the horrible cold dread
Will have fallen on me; I shall be again
Groping my endless way among the tombs.
In a little while! Oh! back ye eager hours,
Why will ye press so to defraud my rest?—

My rest! my rest! Oh! rest that is all pain!
The hours are slow enough for so much pain.
For till the glow of this mysterious light
Glimmering unearthly o'er the worn gray slab—
Woe! woe! its lettering burns into my brain,
I see it though I turn away my eyes,

"LUCILLA A SWEET SOUL ASLEEP IN CHRIST.
AND GLAUCON LOVING HER, MORE LOVING CHRIST"—
Till that pale ghastly glow, like the void rays
That look back to the sun from dead men's eyes,
Fades sudden in the darkness whence it came,
And the fear-anguish once more drives me on,
I, waiting here, perforce must have in mind
That which these Christian fools would call my sin.

    My sin? my glory. Do ye sleep, ye gods,
The guardians and the worshipped of great Rome,
That ye will yield me to the vengeful might
Of this new demon whom these heaven-accursed
Would set above you mocking at your thrones,
This new-found god whose anger I have earned
Because I warred against him, having care
To keep the honours of your temples pure?
Are ye asleep, great gods, or are ye wroth
That in my love for her I would have saved
One who had dared to mock you with her scorn?

    I *would* have saved, Lucilla. But thy fear
Of thy new god was stronger than thy fear
Of even death. Thyself didst choose to die,
It was not I who sent thee with the herd

I hounded from their earths to glut the mart
Of creatures for our shows.   It was not I.
Oh Child, thou knowest I would have had thee live
To love me—Oh! the tender maiden limbs
Wrenched on the rack! torn by the torturer!—
Oh gods! that death!—The panther's dripping jaws!
Their white teeth clotted with—

                   But I did love thee.

Oh best and fairest! Oh! my love, my light,
When saw I love or light except in thee?
What music was there but when thou didst speak?
What beauty was there save what was in thee?
What joy or hope was there in all the earth
That was not thou? What more could the gods give?
And yet, not giving thee, what had they given?
I would have laid my whole life in thy hand,
And found no aim, no will, but to work thine;
I would have died for thee; I would have sinned
Against all laws of heaven or earth, but so
To bring thee one small pleasure; would have met
All agony, yea even this doom, for thee;
All things have done for thee, all things endured
Save but to yield thee, *thou* who wast my all.

And only this thou wouldst! yes, I dare front
Thy pale face rising on me through my dream,
With its accusing eyes, and answer thee :
Thou madest me suffer more than I did thee.

"LUCILLA A SWEET SOUL ASLEEP IN CHRIST."
What is this Christ, that he can give thee sleep
Which is not death? Sleep! shall I call on him
That he may give me sleep? Sleep!—but *he* sleeps,
"GLAUCON MUCH LOVING HER, MORE LOVING
CHRIST."
And shall I sleep with him, I wake with him,
The hated, hated that she did not hate?
Shall I ask mercy from this cross-hung god
Whom Glaucon loved? Gods of our city, no!

Asleep, Lucilla? once I saw thee sleep,
The smile of a pure dream upon thy lips,
Thy light breath heaving thy fair breast as winds
In a mild moonlight surge a sleeping sea,
And but to look on thee was to be calm,
And, for a moment, happy. Now what means
The foolish word asleep? That thou art there
In the clammy earth, a nothing, thou that wast
My all. Would I could feel thee what thou art,

And know thee only as the dead are known
Or else forgotten. But my memory throbs
With such a living sentience that to think
On the once themes is to be my once self.
And I am driven to think of them. And they,
They are thou, Lucilla, thou art made my curse.
I *must* re-live it all—the sudden love,
The months of longing, and the fever waking
When, through my dreams, I knew my one life-hope,
Thy love, was stolen by that boy-beauteous Greek
Whose false voice whispered music in thine ears
That lured thee from the hymnings of our gods.
Through all my soul there stirs the bitter past,
Through all my soul there stirs the happy past
More bitter than the bitter by the touch
Of that great bitterness that curdles all
Its sweetness into gall. I see thy face
Set in the glimmer of that lustrous hair
Rippling all over into dappled waves,
Some like the autumn brambles browning leaf,
And some all shimmering as with burnished gold;
I see thy child-like eyes, blue as the sky,
Dark as the purple thundercloud, their whites

All latticed o'er with little azure veins;
I see the soft pink pallor of thy cheek,
Thy sweet slow smile—Lucilla! Oh! forgive.
Oh! fade strange light, and let my mind again
Lose this sharp knowledge of the sad foregone.
      Ah me! I *must* remember. So my love
Grew a great madness; till thy startled glance
Would shrink from mine in fear and thy dear hand
Would tremble as I touched it—not with love.
No, that was all for *him*—Oh! hate thou him,
If thou canst hate, Lucilla, for thy death;
Call it his deed not mine. Yea, but for him
It had not been. Yea, but for him, thy love,
My curse upon him! I had not been thus:
And, who can tell? I might have slept with thee,
My soul with thine in Christ, or, with me, thou
Have wandered godlike in the happy fields.
      So my strong hate of him through love for thee
Grew ever, flaming through my veins like fire,
Till all my life was but as one black hate,
Till even love for thee seemed like a hate,
Thyself half hateful that thou couldst love him.
My heart burned in me like a poisoned wound

At speech of him, at inward thought of him.—
And how could I once cease to think of him?
Thy name upon my lips was as a curse,
A thousand deepest curses, hurled on him;
My burning lids at night were scorched with sight,
I saw thy smile on him. And in my ears
Was ever sound of thy low voice that spoke
That sweet sweet word of love I heard it speak,
Once while I listened to thine every breath,
And not to me. My fitful fevered sleep
Was mad with dreams of passion and despair,
Yea mad, far worse than all, with dreams of hope
That made the waking sudden misery;
And in the days I writhed, my aching brain
Grew dizzy with its torment. Oh! those days!
That waking to an utter hopelessness,
That dreary sickening loneness at the heart;
And yet to love her, have no wish save her!
And *he* had brought me this. Was not love hate?
Could I love thee and not hate him, thy love?

They say that love can tame the roughest tongue
To soft-voiced sadness, gentle cadences;
Oh! false; there is such power alone in hate.

Hate gave it me, and I could blend my voice
To well-put words of doubt and half belief
And trembling hope to find in that sweet creed
A happy haven for my broken soul.
And thou didst trust me, Oh ! thou guileless ; yea
Thou leddst thy convert to the secret vaults
Where prayers were made to the forbidden god.
And the fond idiots prated brotherhood,
And Glaucon, I was Glaucon's brother too !
And so the poor fools let me come and go
Holding their lives in my hand.

                  They perished : well,
What scathe ? Rome is well rid of such a scum—
Why did they mock our gods, and flout our lives
With their fine preachments ? But she perished too,
Lucilla ! But I meant it not. I dreamed,
Knowing thy tender spirit that would shrink
From even thought of pain to aught that feels,
Knowing thy timid spirit that would quail
At the light terrors its own dread had shaped
In the long shadows of a darkling eve,
I dreamed that thou wouldst cleave unto the grace
My care had made thy right, and buy thy life

At price of one small homage to the gods.

    Alas ! I thought, and gloried in my heart,
Thou wouldst have rested in my shielding arms
Thy weakness and thy fears, too true to doubt
My truth to the vain faith I swore thy god
And thee, who hadst forgotten thou to me
Wast more than truth could give. I thought that
      death
Should part thee from that Glaucon through all time,
And lo ! it weds thee to him through all time;
Thou art with him in death, and I, alone
Look on thy tomb and am thy murderer.

    And yet it had not been if even then,
When thy clear voice scorned at the rites of Jove,
I had been by thee. But my awful doom
Held me a madman in the place of tombs.

    *   *   *   *   *   *   *

The sunshine burst out through a ridge of gloom
And flashed a promise on me where I watched
The answer of the gods ; without a bleat
The victim fell ; the haruspex laughed content
Reading the entrails "See the gods approve.
Go, prosper in thy deed." *Prosper !* I went

Heading my band along the darksome vaults,
They fearless, but I feared not knowing why.
And then in the long cavern's outer gloom
Fronting the dusk arch of the chamber vault
Where their trapped prey were sure, I stayed their
        haste,
Saying, " It fits that I should go before
Alone; because these Christians must not know
Who led you to their den; but pass ye on
In a short half hour where I shall enter now :
For I will seem to pray before their cross. "
      Thee I could see, Lucilla, by the cross,
But swiftly came an awful flame of light—
Then darkness. And I rushed with a great dread
Through the dark maze that gave me no return,
Seized by my everlasting doom.
                  How then,
How comes it that I know that which 1 know?
Was my freed spirit borne among the clouds,
By some strange power, away from my void frame,
Or did I see it as a god might see,
Being far off but having mystic sight?
Woe ! woe ! I look upon the place of shows

.

Red with dark pools, ghastly with mangled limbs
And shapeless dead. I hear the buzz of tongues,
The murmur of a huddled multitude
Mocking the death-pangs, mocking the death-prayers
Of bleeding forms that call upon their Christ.
I hear the eager cry that urges on
The crouching lions glutted with their prey,
Gazing with sullen eyes upon the crowd—
　" Loose more, loose more "—the call rings in my
　　　ears—
　" Loose more ; these make no sport. There are
　　　victims yet."
I see her a fair maiden robed in white,
Standing calm-eyed amid the place of blood,
Standing amid the corpses, not afraid,
Her hand firmed clasped in his all hateful hand—
Lucilla ! *His* Lucilla—never mine.
I hear the echo of her quiet voice,
Oh shuddering hear, " I will not serve nor pray
These dream-born gods, but I will rather die.
My Lord will take me to his rest of love."
I hear the hum of anger through the throng,
I hear low whisperings of pity grow,

And voices call on Glaucon to stand forth
And save his dainty damsel and himself,
Bending with her one moment to great Jove;
And his strong words peal like a trumpet-blast
"Yes, I love her; but more do I love Christ."
And then—I will not see—Oh! save her! save her!
Drag them off her. Am I powerless to reach her
And yet behold?

    And I *must* gaze on this—
Out of some dream? A dream that will return
For ever and for ever!

      Oh! the curse
Is my own earning. Rightly am I doomed.
Her blood, his blood, the blood of many dead
Is on my soul.

    But did she pray for me?
Could even *her* gentleness so well forgive?
It was as if, in a deep pulseless hush
Stiller than sleep, I heard within my heart
While dying she prayed softly to her god
"Oh Lord, forgive him, lead his soul to thee,"
And knew she prayed for me, and loved her prayer,
While for a moment quivered at my heart

A yearning for that rest of love in Christ,
And a quick impulse stirred me to fall down
And call upon her god as she had called.
But he replied, that Glaucon, "Lord, forgive."
And I cried fiercely, clamouring out my wrath,
"Thou Christ, if thou hast any power to hear,
"Hear me, not him—hurl all thy wrath on me,
"I will not be forgiven at his prayer.
"If thou canst hear, hear me."

                              Then I awoke,
And knew myself as one without a soul
Urged by the furies through these endless vaults.
    But this long hour of thought? Why came it
        first?
After what length of days? I cannot judge,
Having in that long fear no breathing time,
Going on and on and on, through ceaseless turns,
In the dead murk and in the ghastly glimmer
Of the far daylight straggling through the shafts,
Going on and on and on towards escape
That never may be reached, my mind a blank
To all save terror and that one vain hope.
It came. I found me as I find me now

Within the place of prayer where that swift flame
Seared me for ever from the lot of men,
And an unnatural radiance, even as now,
Came from the darkness, falling on that tomb—
LUCILLA A SWEET SOUL ASLEEP IN CHRIST,
AND GLAUCON LOVING HER, MORE LOVING CHRIST.
And gazing, there seemed borne upon my mind—
Or did she whisper it from that still tomb?—
That there should be to me each year a space
Of rest and memory enforced beside
Her resting place, that so I might call back
My prayer and "wash away" (the words seem so)
"My sin in weeping and a Saviour's blood,
"And fall asleep in Christ."

                Yea, I would sleep,
Oh! sleep! if I *could* sleep—yea, sleep in Christ
Whom my gods loathe—yea sleep with her in Christ.

    But Glaucon whom I hate—Oh! never rest
Be mine with him, be mine through Giaucon's god.
Hear me, not him, thou Christ.

                The radiance pales—
Is dead. Oh gods! my madness drives me on.
Darkness, all dark—I know not what I say.

BY THE LOOKING-GLASS.

ALONE at last in my room—
How sick I grow of the glitter and din,
Of the lips that smile and the voices that prate
To a ballroom tune for the fashion's sake :
Light and laughters without, but what within?
Are these like me? Do the pleasure and state
Weary them under the seeming they make?—
But I see all through my gloom.

For why should a light young heart
Not leap to a merry moving air,
Not laugh with the joy of the flying hour
And feed upon pleasure just for a while?

But the right of a woman is being fair,
And her heart must starve if she miss that dower,
For how should she purchase the look and the smile?
And I have not had my part.

A girl, and so plain a face!
Once more, as I learn by heart every line
In the pitiless mirror, night by night,
Let me try to think it is not my own.
Come, stranger with features something like mine,
Let me place close by you the tell-tale light;
Can I find in you now some charm unknown,
Only one softening grace?

Alas! it is I, I, I,
Ungainly, common. The other night
I heard one say "Why, she is not so plain.
See, the mouth is shapely, the nose not ill."
If I could but believe his judgement right!
But I try to dupe my eyesight in vain,
For I, who have partly a painter's skill,
I cannot put knowledge by.

He had not fed, as I feed
On beauty, till beauty itself must seem
Me, my own, a part and essence of me,
My right and my being—Why! how am I plain?
I feel as if this were almost a dream
From which I should waken, as it might be,
And open my eyes on beauty again
And know it myself indeed.

Oh idle! oh folly! look,
There, looking back from the glass, is my fate,
A clumsy creature smelling of earth,
What fancy could lend her the angel's wings?
She looks like a boorish peasant's fit mate.
Why! what a mock at the pride of birth,
Fashioned by nature for menial things,
With her name in the red-bound book.

Oh! to forget me a while,
Feeling myself but as one in the throng,
Losing myself in the joy of my youth!
Then surely some pleasure might lie in my reach.

But the sense of myself is ever strong,
And I read in all eyes the bitter truth,
And I fancy scorning in every speech
And mocking in every smile.

Ah! yes, it was so to-night,
And I moved so heavily through the dance,
And answered uncouthly like one ill taught,
And knew that ungentleness seemed on my brow,
While it was but pain at each meeting glance,
For I knew that all who looked at me thought
"How ugly she is! one sees it more now
With the other young faces so bright."

I might be more like the rest,
Like those that laugh with a girlish grace
And make bright nothings an eloquence;
I might seem gentler and softer souled;
But I needs must shape myself to my place,
Softness in me would seem clumsy pretence,
Would they not deem my laughters bold?
I hide in myself as is best.

Do I grow bitter sometimes?
They say it, ah me! and I fear it is true,
And I shrink from that curse of bitterness,
And I pray on my knees that it may not come;
But how should I envy—they say that I do—
All the love which others' young lives may bless?
Because *my* age will be lone in its home
Do I weep at the wedding chimes?

Ah no, for they judge me ill,
Judging me doubtless by that which I look,
Do I not joy for another's delight?
Do I not grieve for another's regret?
And I have been true where others forsook
And kind where others bore hatred and spite,
For there I could think myself welcome—and yet
My care is unpitied still.

Yes, who can think it such pain
Not to be fair "Such a trifling thing."
And "Goodness may be where beauty is not"
And "How weak to sorrow for outward show!"

Ah! if they knew what a poisonful sting
Has this sense of shame, how a woman's lot
Is darkened throughout!—Oh yes I know
How weak—but I know in vain.

    I hoped in vain, for I thought,
When first I grew to a woman's days,
Woman enough to feel what it means
To be a woman and not be fair,
That I need not sigh for the voice of praise
And the beauty's triumph in courtly scenes
Where she queens with her maiden-royal air,
Ah! and so worshipped and sought.

But I, oh my dreaming! deemed
With a woman's yearning and faith in love,
With a woman's faith in her lovingness,
That that joy might brighten on me, even me,
For which all the force of my nature strove,
Joy of daily smiles and voices that bless,
And one deeper other love it might be—
Hush, *that* was wrong to have dreamed.

I thank God, I have not loved,
Loved as one says it whose life has gone out
Into another's for evermore,
Loved as I know what love might be
Writhing but living through poison of doubt,
Drinking the gall of the sweetness before,
Drinking strange deep strength from the bitter lee—
Love, love in a falsehood proved !

Loving him on to the end,
Through the weary weeping hours of the night,
Through the wearier laughing hours of the day ;
Knowing him less than the love I gave,
But this one fond dream left my life for its light
To do him some service and pass away ;
Not daring, for sin, to think of the grave
Lest it seemed the only friend.

Thank God that it was not so,
And I have my scatheless maidenly pride,
But it might have been—for did he not speak
With that slow sweet cadence that seemed made
        deep

By a meaning—Hush! he has chosen his bride.
Oh! happy smile on her lips and her cheek,
My darling! And I have no cause to weep,
I have not bowed me so low.

But would he have wooed in vain?
Would not my heart have leaped to his will,
If he had not changed?—How, *changed* do I say?
Was I not mocked with an idle thought,
Dreaming and dreaming so foolishly still?
By the sweet glad smile and the winning way
And the grace of beauty alone is love bought.
He woo me! Am I not plain?

But yet I was not alone
To fancy I might be something to him.
They thought it, I know, though it seems so wild
Now, in this bitterer Now's hard light.
Vain that I was! could his sight grow dim?
How could he love me? But she, when she smiled
Once, the first once, by her beauty's right
Had made all his soul her own.

It is well that no busy tongue
Has vexed her heart with those bygone tales.
But I think he fears he did me some wrong,
I see him watch me at times, and his cheek
Crimsons a little, a little pales,
If his eye meets mine for a moment long.
But he need not fear, I am not so weak
Though I *am* a woman and young.

I had not grown to my love,
Though it might have been. And I give no blame:
Nothing was spoken to bind him to me,
Nothing had been that could make him think
My heart beat stronger and fast when he came,
And if he *had* loved me, was he not free,
When the fancy passed, to loose that vague link
That only such fancy wove?

No he has done no such ill
But that I can bear it, nor shame in my heart
To call him my brother and see her his,
The one little pearl that gleams through our gloom:

He has no dishonour to bar them apart.
I loving her so, am rested in this ;
Else I would speak though I spoke her doom,
Though grief had the power to kill.

When she came a while ago,
My young fair sister bright with her bloom,
Back to a home which is little glad,
I thought "Here is one who should know no care,
A little wild bird flown into a room
From its far free woods; will she droop and grow
　　　　　sad ?
But, here even, love smiles upon one so fair.
And I too might feel that glow."

But now she will fly away !
Ah me ! and I love her so deep in my heart
And worship her beauty as he might do.
If I could but have kept her a little time !
Ah she will go ! So the sunbeams depart
That brightened the winter's sky into blue,
And the dews of the chill dusk freeze into rime,
And cold cold mists hang grey.

I think she loved me till now—
Nay doubtless she loves me quietly yet,
But his lightest fancy is more, far more,
To her than all the love that I live.
But I cannot blame (as if love were a debt)
That, though I love, he is held far before;
And is it not well that a bride should give
All, all her heart with her vow?

But ah, if I smiled more sweet
And spoke more soft as one fairer could,
Had not love indeed been more surely mine?
Folly to say that a woman's grace
Is only strong o'er a man's light mood!
Even the hearts of the nearest incline
With a gentler thought to the lovely face,
And the winning eyes that entreat.

But I—yes flicker pale light,
Fade into darkness and hide it away,
The poor dull face that looks out from the glass,
Oh wearily wearily back to me!

Yes, I will sleep, for my wild thoughts stray
Weakly, selfishly—yes let them pass,
Let self and this sadness of self leave me free,
Lost in the peace of the night.

TOO LATE.

WHAT dead!—And I was only yesternight
    Revolving eager schemes for my redemption
    Out of these depths where I have plunged
        myself,
Thinking I saw her with her earnest eyes
Smile like the angels on the penitent.
And then, Oh God! just in my hopefulness,
Then did the arrow pierce me—"she may die."
But could I think that such an agony
Could come upon me?—nay 'twas past belief.
How *could* she die?

             Through the wild wintry night
The crashing train rushed onwards, and I groaned
Between my teeth "On! on! we scarcely move."

And the white snow-shapes, peering thro' the
    gloom,
Took forms like ghosts that beckoned, beckoned
    on ;
And the long shrieks and hissings and the clangings,
As we whirred on, were sobs and bitter wails
And hoarse strange voices crying " she may die ! "
And then I moaned aloud " She *cannot* die !
" I *will* not have her die ! "

                                            I find her dead !
Dead ! oh my Amy dead !

                                           Too late ! too late !
I cannot kiss her pallid lips to life
For one last long farewell.   Look the blue lids
Are sealed upon the eyes ; they will not rise
For one last gaze to show she loved me still.
I did not close them.   'Twas not on *my* breast
Her dying head was rested in that anguish
The last life gave her—ah ! it gave so many !
It gave ? *I* gave ! Oh but one little breath,
One moment of forgiveness, and I might
Kneel down and pray beside her patiently,
Kneel down and rise a less unworthy man.

Yes she is dead—but do you say I killed her?
Did you fold those thin hands upon her breast
That I might see how wasted they had grown?
Ah me! the ring sits loose on that shrunk finger.
If I might dare to take it from her now,
And wear it for a conscience, just to preach
The lessons my dulled conscience trips at!

                        No

I am not worthy.   Let it go with her.
I will remember that in a lone grave
My wife is wearing still her wedding ring,
That I may know she is my own.

                     Ah! child,

Fresh from the meadows, lily-hearted child,
If only you had never been my own,
If I had left you in your lowliness,
I should have lost your glory on my life
But should have had this worst remorse the less,
And you would still be singing in your home.
Oh! what had I to do to drag you down
To my unworth, and fancy, braggart fool!
Because I shrieked my first in a tall room
Panelled with portraitures of better men

Than I who shame their race, and your mazed
    eyes
Were opened on a dingy white-washed wall,
That I could raise you—I, who was more far
Beneath you than I'd sunk from my first self.
Oh dreamer that I was! I took from you,
My little one, your simple happiness
And thought I could replace it from a heart
That only dreamed the thing it should have been.
And now you lie there, ghastly white and cold,
And the gold locks I used to tease droop down
By a thin cheek and round a wasted throat,
And you are dead.
            Oh! if you could but hear!
They of the strange new faith the Swedish saint
Dreamed in his trances say that for three days
Death is not where it seems, and the stiff corpse
Might hear and understand the living still.
Oh! if it could but be! if you could hear
And know I ask forgiveness thus, oh thus
Weeping. No you smile on a changeless smile
Of bliss ineffable; you would not smile
If you could see me weep, hear my wild sorrow.

You lie there stony. I can never think
I gave you so much comfort at the last
As just to ask forgiveness. 'Tis too late;
You are gone from me. Oh! too late! too late!